Lehr- und Handbücher zu Sprachen und Kulturen

Herausgegeben von
José Vera Morales und Martin M. Weigert

Bisher erschienene Werke:

Communication in Business

Von
Birgit Pawelzik

R. Oldenbourg Verlag München Wien

Bibliografische Information Der Deutschen Bibliothek

Die Deutsche Bibliothek verzeichnet diese Publikation in der Deutschen
Nationalbibliografie; detaillierte bibliografische Daten sind im Internet
über <http://dnb.ddb.de> abrufbar.

© 2005 Oldenbourg Wissenschaftsverlag GmbH
Rosenheimer Straße 145, D-81671 München
Telefon: (089) 45051-0
www.oldenbourg-verlag.de

Gedruckt auf säure- und chlorfreiem Papier
Gesamtherstellung: Druckhaus „Thomas Müntzer" GmbH, Bad Langensalza

ISBN 3-486-57705-0

INTRODUCTION

1. How has communication changed over the past decade?

The invention of the World Wide Web in 1990 by Tim Berners-Lee can be regarded as an important turning point in communication. This gave the impetus to an extremely rapid development towards electronic mail, both in business and at home. Starting with approx 5% in the 1990s, emails now account for 90% of all communication, the remaining 10% being composed of fax transmissions or letters.

Time is money. These days, you can send emails anywhere on the planet regardless of time, space or the price of long-distance phone calls. Yet, emailing not only saves time and money, in an indirect way, it also influences our lifestyle. A completely new simplified style, with open punctuation, and frequent use of abbreviations, has superseded the traditional, very formal style of business letters. Thus, communication has become easy, fast and more personal.

2. What makes good communication?

Always having the right expression at the ready! **Communication in Business** will teach you the right words for both oral and written communication.

If you are already working and want to improve your communication skills in English, **Communication in Business** may serve as the latest reference book.

Whether you want to start preparing for the world of work or for learning at home alongside a full-time career **Communication in Business** will help you to gain an insight into how to communicate effectively, correctly and in a modern way in the most important situations in everyday business.

Accompanied by essential background information on commerce and foreign trade, **Communication in Business** covers the following domains: oral communication on the phone, at meetings and presentations or on visits to business partners, and written communication in the form of emails, letters and job applications.

3. What makes this book different?

The wheel of time turns quickly. Based on the latest research into business correspondence and communication, **Communication in Business** analyses what makes a good correspondent work efficiently and a good speaker talk successfully. **Communication in Business** identifies the key skills employed in the world of commercial business. Therefore, research is mainly based on information and experience gained in international companies to reflect the latest practical usage. Extensive Internet research has also provided up-to-date commercial background information. There is an appendix of the latest developments.

Learning in stories. It is a well-known fact that our brains remember developments more easily than a simple series of facts. Therefore, email and letter extracts in **Communication in Business** deal with famous companies and follow case studies that develop throughout the book. However, in all the case studies, names of business partners, prices, terms and conditions are imaginary.

4. How to use this book?

Communication in Business is written in British English and all email and letter extracts are given with open punctuation to reflect the state of the art. An appendix shows the difference in spelling between British English (BE) and American English (AE). Email or letter extracts have been marked by corresponding flags to show if they are drafted in BE or AE. Text components which are not written in BE are marked (AE). All words and expressions which are underlined can be found in the attached glossary arranged in alphabetical order. Short explanations of essential terms are given in the footnotes.

Important background information regarding commercial terms is always given at the very stage where the terms arise. This helps to create a sound basis on which you can easily follow the successive units. Consequently, some units are longer than others depending on the volume of background information provided.

Finally, an up-to-date listing of common abbreviations in use in commercial trade is attached.

Starting softly. **Communication in Business** is divided into 23 units with increasing degrees of difficulty. Gradually, you will build up your skills, competence and confidence.

- Units 1-3 show you the basics of what you should know before going into detail.
- Units 4-6 teach you the typical standard phrases you should be able to use automatically on the phone, at business meetings or in emails.
- Units 7-20 lead you continuously through the traditional commercial sections.
- Unit 21 helps you to apply successfully for jobs or placements.
- Unit 22 -23 give you clear structures to easily establish your concept in presentations and meetings.

Acknowledgements

I would like to thank the following persons for their valuable contributions to **Communication in Business:**

Lothar Schmidt and Edite Carvalho at Durable, Helen Nurse of the University of Applied Sciences Cologne, Dorota Pawlucka of the University of Dortmund, Regine Seuren at Hunt & Palmer Ltd, Katja Robben, Aphrodite Fischer and Christine Dollmann.

Most of all, I would like to thank my husband for his patience and support.

Birgit Pawelzik

Author

Before and after graduating from the University of Applied Sciences Cologne as a translator, Birgit Pawelzik worked for many years in international business, especially in export departments, credit agencies and translation departments. She has also taught English commercial correspondence in Germany and is an experienced trainer and presenter.

UNIT 1   BASICS I WRITING BUSINESS LETTERS

1.1 Key facts

In recent times, most of the correspondence in international trade is handled by email since this is the quickest and cheapest way of communication. However, in certain cases it is still necessary to write a letter, eg when sending a contract or <u>samples</u> and <u>patterns</u>.
Therefore, we will focus on the following:

- Layout
- Punctuation
- Parts of a business letter

1.1.1 Layout

Nowadays business letters are written fully blocked. **Block letters** have every line <u>flush with the left margin</u>.

1.1.1.2 Form of a business letter

(1) LETTERHEAD
Company address, Email, phone, fax, website
(2) COMPANY REFERENCE NUMBER/INITIALS
(3) DATE LINE
(4) ADDRESSEE
(5) SUBJECT LINE
(6) SALUTATION
(7) TEXT
(8) COMPLIMENTARY CLOSE
(9) SIGNATURE BLOCK
(10) ENCLOSURE
(11) CC

1.1.2 Punctuation

You are free to choose between open and <u>full punctuation</u>, though it is worth noting that with the advent of word processing <u>open punctuation</u> is now widely used.

Open punctuation: all punctuation marks are omitted except full stops at the end of a sentence.

Full punctuation: punctuation marks are placed after the following:
- Date
- Salutation
- Complimentary close
- Abbreviations
- Initials

1.1.2.1 Overview punctuation

OPEN PUNCTUATION	FULL PUNCTUATION
Mr S M Brown	Mr. S.M. Brown
25 November 2005	25 November, 2005
Dear Mr Smith	Dear Mr. Smith,
Sincerely	Sincerely,
Main Street No 234	Main Street No. 234
J Brown	J. Brown
eg	e.g.
am	a.m.
etc	etc.
Co Ltd	Co. Ltd.

1.1.3 Parts of a business letter

(1) Usually, the **letterhead** is pre-printed and indicates the company's logo, full address, phone and fax number, email address and homepage. It can be aligned to the left, right or centre of a page.

(2) The company's **reference number** and/or **initials** identify who in the company sent the letter. Generally, the writer's initials are in all capitals, followed by a slash, and then followed by the typist's initials in lowercase letters.

TH/pj

(3) The **date** is written differently in BE and AE, this may cause confusion when written only in figure form. For this reason, it is often better to write the date in full:

BE	AE
day-month-year 14-10-05	month-day-year 10-14-05
14 October 2005	October 14, 2005

(4) The **name and the address of the <u>addressee</u>** are indicated. If you write to the attention of a person, the name and the function of the person is mentioned **before** the company name of the addressee. When writing to a particular department, the department is mentioned **after** the company name in the address.

Ms Janet Read Purchasing Manager Twinings Ltd South Way Andover Hampshire SP10 5AQ* Great Britain	Reebok International Ltd Sales Department 1895 J W Foster Boulevard Canton, MA 02021* USA

*In GB you have a <u>post code</u> and in the USA you have a <u>zip code</u>.

(5) In German and American letters, the <u>subject line</u> is placed **before** the <u>salutation</u>, however, in Great Britain it is different.

BE	AE
Dear Sirs	China Agreement
China Agreement	Gentlemen

(6) The correct <u>salutation</u> must be used with the <u>complimentary close</u>. Once again there are differences in BE and AE:

BE SALUTATION	BE COMPLIMEN- TARY CLOSE	AE SALUTATION	AE COMPLIMEN- TARY CLOSE
Formal			
Dear Sirs	Yours faithfully	Gentlemen	Sincerely
Dear Sir or Madam	Yours faithfully	Ladies and Gentlemen	Sincerely
Dear Mr Green	Yours sincerely	Dear Mr Gates	Sincerely
Dear Ms Brown	Yours sincerely	Dear Ms Tucker	Sincerely
Friends			
Dear David	With best wishes/ With kind regards	Dear Jim	With best wishes/ With kind regards

Mrs is used for married women only.
Ms is used for married or unmarried women, and should be used if the addressee's marital status is unclear.

(7) The **text of the letter** should be drafted according to the *KISS*-principle: **Keep It** Short and Simple! There must be one clear line space between paragraphs to divide the text into manageable sections.

(8) The **complimentary close** must conform to the salutation, see chart **(6)** salutation.

(9) The <u>**signature block**</u> contains the signature of the writer, the full typed name of the writer, and the position of the writer. The company name is optional.

Reebok International Ltd
Tony Hancock
Tony Hancock
Sales Manager

(10) Should <u>**enclosures**</u> be made, such as catalogues and price lists, notations appear directly under the signature block.

Enc

(11) <u>**Courtesy copy**</u> notations show the distribution of the letter and are placed below the enclosure notations. All individuals receiving the letter in addition to the addressee are listed.

CC Ms Emma Green, Marketing Manager

<u>Continuation page headings</u>

Continuation pages contain the name of the addressee, the date and the page number.

NIKE Inc
October 14, 2005
Page 2

1.2 Faxes

Faxes and letters are about the same regarding form and layout. Most companies have standardised fax forms where the necessary data is to be entered before writing the text of the fax.

1.2.1 Fax header

FACSIMILE TRANSMISSION

Fax no:	+49 231 75 68 11 23	From:	**Tony Hancock**
Attention of:	**Volker Zoellner**	Date:	**August 20, 2005**
Company:	**Sportarena, Germany**	Time:	**09:08**
No of pages:	**1**	(including this cover sheet) Please telephone if you do not receive all pages	

Dear Mr Zoellner

Following our recent telephone conversations, we are pleased to confirm the following information as the basis of our future cooperation:

Payment terms: 30 days, 2%, 60 days net
Delivery: FOB German port
Delivery date: within two weeks from receipt of order
Prices: to be agreed upon

We trust that you will find the above to be in good order and we look forward to receiving your enquiries[1] soon.

Best regards

Tony Hancock
Reebok International Ltd, USA

**1895 J W Foster Boulevard Canton,
MA 02021   USA
Phone: 1-800-934-3566   Fax: 1-800-934-3455
Internet: www.reebok.com**

[1] Enquiries are also spelled inquiries. However, the term enquiry is more common.

UNIT 2   BASICS II WRITING EMAILS

2.1 Key facts

The overriding principle when writing an email is *KISS*, ie **Keep It Short and Simple**. Your message should be short, simple and clear! Therefore, we will focus on

- Length
- Sentences
- Words

Length of an email

There is an art to being as brief as possible and as long as necessary. Of course, the length should be appropriate to the subject matter, however, try to be as concise as possible!

Sentences

Writing emails is like texting messages. They must be short and easy to understand. Therefore, long and woolly phrases should be omitted.

Words

When writing an email every word should be justified. Try to avoid long and scientific words if there is a short or common alternative.

2.2 Letters and emails in comparison

LETTER	EMAIL
Formal language	Informal language
Tendency to write longer sentences	Sentences: according to the *KISS*-principle
Tendency to use long, foreign/ scientific words	Short and everyday words
Subject heading has to be placed correctly, ie BE: **after** the <u>salutation</u> AE: **before** the salutation.	Email software provides space for subject heading and prompts one if it is forgotten.
cc has to be placed at the end of the letter.	Email software provides space for cc.

LETTER	EMAIL
Formal salutation:	**Informal salutation:**
Dear Sir or Madam	Dear Richard
Dear Ms Green	Hello Nick
Ladies and Gentlemen	Hi David
	Dear Colleagues
Formal <u>complimentary close</u>:	**Informal <u>complimentary close</u>:**
Yours faithfully (BE)	Best regards
Yours sincerely (BE)	Best wishes
Sincerely (AE)	Regards
	Have a good day.
	Have a nice weekend.
Enclosure	Attachment
Little use of abbreviations	Much use of abbreviations

UNIT 3   BASICS III USING COMMON PHRASES

3.1 Key facts

When writing emails or letters it is important to use a suitable opening or closing phrase depending on the circumstances. The most common phrases are mentioned below.

3.2 Common phrases
3.2.1 Giving information

This is to inform you that …

> *Mr Hancock is retiring at the end of October this year. His successor will be Jim Thomson.*

Just a quick note to advise you that …

> *we have put the directions and a site map on our website.*

I am writing to let you know about …

> *our new project in China. If you need anything else, please let me know.*

3.2.2 Replying to a letter or email

Thank you for …

> *your letter of 15 May. Please note that your request is receiving attention. As soon as we have got the information required, we will contact you.*

In reply to …

> *your email, please find attached our new sales letter. Please let me have your comments soon.*

Referring to …

> *your last email, please note our <u>General Terms and Conditions</u> specified on our website www.twinings.com.*
> *Should you have any further questions please do not hesitate to contact us.*

3.2.3 Giving favourable information

We are pleased to announce that ...

> *Mr Brown has been appointed to the position of Export Manager of our company.*

We are delighted to inform you that ...

> *Twinings will be <u>exhibiting</u> at ANUGA[2] Food Tec Cologne from 4 April to 7 April 2005. We would be pleased to welcome you to our stand.*

We are glad to...

> *introduce ourselves as one of the leading exporters of tea.*

3.2.4 Giving unfavourable information

We regret to inform you that ...

> *Mr Miller left our company at the end of June. Ms Susan Little is now in charge of customer support.*

We are sorry to tell you that ...

> *the hp printer requested by you is no longer available. However, we could substitute a similar product, our hp 925c printer, at the same price.*

We kindly ask you for ...

> *immediate payment of our <u>invoice</u> no 2367 dated 8 July 2005 for € 2,500.50.*

---

[2] International trade fair for food technology

3.2.5 Attaching files or enclosing documentation

Following our emails recently, I am sending you enclosed …

> *the brochure about our new "speed programme" in English. Please let me know if it would be useful to have it translated into German and French.*

Further to our exchange of emails last week …

> *I am attaching a copy of the agreement that is currently in place between hp and ALDI, Germany. Please let me know if this document can be adopted on the German market.*

Attached please find …

> *a copy of the confirmation sent to our sales representative in Florida.*

3.2.6 Asking for comments

Please let me have your comments on …

> *the attached version of our hp mini leaflet. If anyone can come up with better headings please let me know.*

Let me know what …

> *you think about it.*

Please contact me …

> *if you have any comments or suggestions.*

3.2.7 Apologising for delays in answering

Sorry, it has taken a while to …

> *send you the <u>quotation</u> but my client arrived just after we spoke and our meeting has just finished.*

Sorry, it took so long, but …

> *David wanted to approve it and he is quite busy.*

Sorry for …

> *the late reply, we just noticed your message.*

3.2.8 Closing letters or emails

I look forward to …

hearing from you soon.

If you have any further questions, …

please do not hesitate to contact me.

If you have any comments, changes or additions to …

text or layout, please let me know asap.

3.2.9 Closing emails

If you have any questions, …

please phone me.

Hope this helps.

Many thanks and have a nice weekend.

UNIT 4   MAKING SUCCESSFUL PHONE CALLS

4.1 Key facts

Besides writing emails or texting messages, answering the phone is the most common form of communication. Therefore, excellent telephone skills are vital in business. Whether you are the caller or the callee, ie the person being called, you should be well trained for the most frequent situations on the phone. Therefore, we will focus on the following:

- Greeting correctly
- Introducing
- Checking the caller's name
- Finding the right person/department
- Enquiring about the reason for calling
- Getting connected
- Apologising
- Offering help
- Leaving a message
- Solving communication problems
- Dialling the wrong number

4.1.2   Greeting correctly

Callee: Reebok International Ltd. Good Morning, Tony Hancock speaking. How can I help you?
or
Callee: Reebok International Ltd. Good Afternoon, Tony Hancock speaking. Can I help you?

4.1.3   Introducing

Caller: This is Volker Zöllner of Sportarena, Cologne, Germany.
or
Caller: Volker Zöllner here. Good morning.

4.1.4   Checking the caller's name

Callee: May I have your name, please?

or

Callee: Who's calling, please?

or

Callee: Who shall I say is calling?

or

Callee: I'm sorry, Sir. I didn't quite catch your name.

4.1.5   Finding the right person/department

Caller: Is that Tony Hancock?

Callee: Yes, speaking.

or

Caller: I'd like to speak to Mr Hancock.

or

Caller: Could you put me through to Mr Hancock?

or

Caller: Is Mr Hancock there?

Callee: Yes, he has just come in.

or

Callee: Do you mean Mr Tony Hancock or Mr Jack Hancock?

or

Callee: Do you know the extension number?

4.1.6   Enquiring about the reason for calling

Callee: May I ask the reason for calling?

or

Callee: May I ask the purpose of your call?

4.1.7   Getting connected

Callee: Hold the line, please. I'll put you through.

or

Callee: I'm trying to connect you. Could you hold on, please?

4.1.8 Apologising

Callee: Sorry to have kept you waiting.

or

Callee: I'm sorry, but the line is busy at the moment. Would you mind calling back in half an hour?

or

Callee:I'm sorry, but the line is engaged. Would you like to hold on? I'll try again.

or

Callee: I'm afraid, …

Mr Hancock is not at his desk at the moment.

he is speaking on another line.

he is not available just now.

he is in a meeting at the moment.

he is not in the office today.

he is on a business trip.

he is expected back on Wednesday.

he is on paternity leave.

he is on sick leave. Ms Hall is covering for him in the meantime. I'll put you through.

or

Callee: Sorry, …

you got cut off. This is a bad line.

you got disconnected.

4.1.9 Offering help

Callee: Is it urgent?

or

Callee: You can call him on his mobile.

or

Callee: Would you like to speak to someone else?

4.1.10   Leaving a message

Caller: Can I leave a message, please?

or

Caller: Can you take a message for me?

Callee: Yes of course. Let me just get a pen. - OK, I'm ready.

or

Caller: Could you pass on a message for me?

or

Caller: Would you please tell Mr Hancock to call me back?

or

Caller: Would you please tell Mr Hancock that Volker Zöllner of Sportarena Cologne has called?

Callee: Can I get him to call you back?

or

Callee: I'll get him to call you back asap.

or

Callee: I'll make sure he gets the message.

4.1.11   Solving communication problems

Callee: Sorry, I missed that.

or

Callee: Could you repeat that, please?

or

Callee: Could you speak up a bit, please? I'm afraid the line is bad.

or

Callee: Could you speak a bit more slowly, please?

or

Callee: Could you please spell that for me?

4.1.12   Dialling the wrong number/person

Caller: Sorry, I must have dialled the wrong number.
Callee: Sorry, this is the wrong department.

or
Callee: Sorry, this is the wrong extension.

or
Callee: You've got through to the wrong number.

or
Callee: Sorry, you are speaking to the wrong person. I'm the
Area Manager for Asia. Mr Smith is responsible for the
European market. I'll put you through.

4.2 Spelling over the phone
4.2.1 Telephone alphabet

The telephone alphabet helps to avoid misunderstandings. This is the most commonly used alphabet in the UK:

A	**for**	Andrew	**N**	**for**	Nelly
B		Benjamin	**O**		Oliver
C		Charlie	**P**		Peter
D		David	**Q**		Queenie
E		Edward	**R**		Robert
F		Frederick	**S**		Sugar
G		George	**T**		Tom
H		Harry	**U**		Uncle
I		Isaac	**V**		Victor
J		Jack	**W**		William
K		King	**X**		Xmas
L		Lucy	**Y**		Yellow
M		Mary	**Z**		Zebra

4.2.2 Numbers

Figures are usually indicated in groups of three:

241 356 123   two four one   three five six   one two three

205	BE: two oh five	AE: two zero five
2005	BE: two double oh five	AE: two zero zero five
2335	BE: two double three five	AE: two three three five

4.2.3 Email addresses:

@	is given as	**at**
.	is given as	**dot**
:	is given as	**colon**
/	is given as	**slash or stroke**
-	is given as	**minus, hyphen or dash**
_	is given as	**underscore**

eg	john miller@fh-koeln.de
	john miller **at** f h **minus** k o e l n **dot** d e

4.2.4 Internet addresses:

www.fh-koeln.de
double u   double u   double u   **dot**   f h   **minus**   k o e l n   **dot**   d e

4.3 Golden rules

1. Answer the phone quickly!
2. Always give your name!
3. Greet the caller politely. (Smile, you can hear it!)
4. Listen to what the caller is saying!
5. Show interest and understanding!
6. Don't give any one-word answers!
7. Try to be helpful!
8. Make sure you pass on any message you take!
9. Make sure you follow-up on any promises you have made!
10. Double check times, dates and telephone numbers!

4.4 Tasks

4.4.1 Practise makes perfect

Practise your telephone skills with your neighbour, friend or colleague. Follow the above situations on the phone.

4.4.2 Practise makes perfect

Practise spelling your name, email-address and, if available, your internet address.

4.4.3 Fill in the missing prepositions

1. This is Volker Zöllner ... Sportarena, Cologne, Germany.
2. Could you put me through ... Mr Hancock?
3. May I ask the reason ... calling?
4. May I ask the purpose ... your call?
5. Could you hold ... ?
6. Could you pass ... a message ... me?
7. Sorry, you got cut ... .
8. Sorry, you are speaking ... the wrong person.
9. He is ... a meeting at the moment.
10. I'm afraid Mr Hancock is not ... his desk.

UNIT 5   MAKING ARRANGEMENTS

5.1 Key facts

Nowadays, most arrangements are made by phone or email. Therefore, we will focus on common phrases when:

Step 1   Making arrangements
Step 2   Arranging a meeting point
Step 3   Confirming arrangements
Step 4   Changing arrangements

5.2 Step 1   Making arrangements

I'm calling to …

> *arrange a meeting with Ms Langer and Ms Read.*
> *When would suit you best?*
> *How about Monday 19 July?*
> *Is 10 am OK?*

I'm ringing to …

> *arrange a time for an interview at Reebok International Ltd.*
> *Is Wednesday July 21 convenient for you?*
> *What about 11 am?*

I'm writing to …

> *arrange a time for your visit to Twinings, Andover next week.*
> *When would suit you best? Monday 19 or Friday 23 July, at 3 pm?*
> *Please let me know asap which day is convenient.*

5.3 Step 2   Arranging a meeting point

Should we …
>   *arrange for someone to <u>pick you up</u> from Düsseldorf*
>   *airport?*

Should we …
>   *collect you from Cologne main station?*

Where should we …
>   *meet? How about the meeting point at Düsseldorf airport?*
>   *Please send me an email by tomorrow to confirm this.*

What about meeting …
>   *directly on platform 3?*
>   *Please send me your confirmation by 3 pm today.*

or

Would you …
>   *arrange for someone to pick me up from Düsseldorf*
>   *airport?*

Could you …
>   *collect me from Cologne main station?*

Meet me …
>   *at the meeting point at Düsseldorf airport.*

See you …
>   *tomorrow on platform 3.*

5.4 Step 3   Confirming arrangements

I'm just ringing to …

> *confirm my visit. Monday 19 July at 3 pm suits me. See you then.*

I am writing …

> *on behalf of Ms Langer to confirm her visit on Monday 19 July 2005.*
> *Could you make a hotel reservation for her from Monday 19 to Tuesday 20 July 2005? Thanks for your prompt reply.*

This is to …

> *confirm the visit of Mr Hancock and Mr Zöllner on Wednesday July 21, 2005 at 3 pm to your <u>premises</u>. Could you arrange a <u>factory tour</u>? Please let me know.*

I would like to …

> *confirm my visit to Twinings Ltd. I'd prefer Wednesday 21 July 2005 at 3 pm.*
> *I look forward to meeting you.*

5.5 Step 4   Changing arrangements

I'm just calling about …

> *our sales training tomorrow. Sorry, but I can't make it. We have a meeting in the afternoon, and you never know how long it will last.*

I'm afraid, …

> *I can't manage our meeting next Monday but Tuesday would be fine. Can you make it?*

Unfortunately, …

> *I can't attend the business conference next week. I will be on a business trip to Europe at that time.*

5.6 Tasks

5.6.1 Practise makes perfect

Practise the four steps of "making arrangements" with your neighbour, friend or colleague.

5.6.2 Fill in the missing prepositions

1. I'm ringing to arrange a meeting … Mr Gates and Mr Jackson.
2. I'm calling to arrange a time … an interview … Microsoft Corp.
3. Is Monday 3 June convenient … you?
4. I'm writing to arrange a time … your visit … our company next week.
5. Should we arrange … someone to pick you up … the airport?
6. Could you collect me … the main station?
7. Please send me your confirmation … tomorrow.
8. I'm writing … behalf … Mr Gates to confirm his visit … Friday, November 11.
9. Could you arrange … a demonstration … the new software programme?
10. I look forward … meeting you.

UNIT 6   WELCOMING BUSINESS PARTNERS

6.1 Key facts

In order to make business partners and contacts feel welcome and comfortable, small talk is an important communication skill. Conducting these light and casual conversations successfully could turn an interested businessman into a key customer. Being aware of this essential skill, we will focus on the following steps:

Step 1   Greeting
Step 2   Breaking the ice
Step 3   Getting down to business
Step 4   Coming to an end
Step 5   Taking leave

6.1.2 Situation:

Mr Hancock, Sales Manager of Reebok International Ltd, USA calls on **Mr Zöllner**, Purchasing Manager of Sportarena, Köln, to discuss the cooperation for the next business year.

6.2 Step 1   Greeting

Mr Zöllner:	Good morning Mr Hancock. I'm Volker Zöllner. Pleased to meet you personally. We've only had the pleasure of phoning or mailing so far, haven't we?
Mr Hancock:	The pleasure is mine.
Mr Zöllner:	Please have a seat. May I offer you something to drink? Coffee, tea, water or anything else?
Mr Hancock:	Thank you, a coffee would be fine.

6.3 Step 2   Breaking the ice

Mr Zöllner: How was your flight to Cologne?
Mr Hancock: It started very pleasantly but shortly before reaching Cologne it became quite <u>bumpy</u>.
Mr Zöllner: Is this your first visit to Germany?
Mr Hancock: No, I was here last year, too, but just in Munich.
Mr Zöllner: How long are you going to stay?
Mr Hancock: One week in total, two days in Cologne, two days in Stuttgart and three days in Munich.
Mr Zöllner: Oh, that's fine. Would you like to join me for dinner tonight? I could take you to a <u>stroll</u> around the ancient city of Cologne and have dinner in a typical local brewery.
Mr Hancock: Thank you. That sounds good. The ancient city of Cologne is great. Yesterday evening I got a <u>glimpse</u> of it.

6.4 Step 3   Getting down to business

Mr Hancock: Since you are a bit <u>tight with time</u>, let's come to the point. You showed special interest in ...
expanding our Reebok running collection at the ISPO[3].

or

Mr Hancock: You expressed interest in …
our new our new Reebok soccer shoes and announced orders for larger quantities. What quantities are we talking about?

or

Mr Zöllner: Since you were interested in a <u>factory tour</u>, …
we have arranged for one at 11 am. The tour will take approx 45 minutes. So we have got about one hour to discuss our future ooperation first.

or

[3] International trade fair for sports goods and sports wear

> **Mr Hancock:** Well, last time we spoke you complained about ...
> *the quality of our new running shoe. You know we have made a considerable effort to improve our quality. Have you had any problems since?*
>
> or
>
> **Mr Zöllner:** After our conversation I would like to show you around our company. That brings me to ...
> *your brand new product, your Reebok Minicomp, the running shoe featuring individual <u>adjustments</u> to be made at the push of button by means of a minicomputer. When will sample shoes be available?*

6.5 Step 4   Coming to an end

> **Mr Zöllner:** Well, it's time for our factory tour ...
> *As already discussed before, you will send us the necessary details next week and we will <u>submit</u> you an offer based on the terms agreed upon.*
>
> or
>
> **Mr Zöllner:** Well, it's time for lunch now, isn't it?
> *We can continue our conversation at lunch.*
>
> or
>
> **Mr Hancock:** Well, I'm glad we could agree on ...
> *the new <u>terms of payment</u> and delivery. My personal assistant, Ms Jones, will send you the agreement within the next two days. Thank you for devoting so much of your precious time.*

6.6 Step 5   Taking leave

Mr Hancock: I'm afraid I've got to leave now to get my connecting flight to Munich.

Mr Zöllner: Oh what a pity you have to go already. It was a pleasure meeting you. Should you come over to Germany next year, I would be very pleased to welcome you at Sportarena again. Our driver will take you to the airport now. Good bye. Have a pleasant journey back home!

or

Mr Hancock: I'm afraid I've got a train to catch.

Mr Zöllner: Well, I mustn't keep you. It is always a pleasure having you here at Sportarena. Thank you for visiting our company. Shall I call a taxi to take you to the airport?

or

Mr Hancock: I'm afraid I've got to leave now. I've got two more engagements today.

Mr Zöllner: It was a pleasure meeting you personally. Have a nice day. See you tonight for dinner. I'll <u>pick you up</u> at 8 pm at the reception of your hotel.

6.7 Tasks
6.7.1 Practise makes perfect

Practise the five steps of "welcoming a business partner" with your neighbour, friend or colleague.

6.7.2 Fill in the missing prepositions

1. May I offer you something ... drink?
2. Is this your first visit ... Germany?
3. Would you like to join us ... dinner tonight?
4. We could take you ... a stroll around the ancient city of Cologne and have dinner ... a typical local brewery.
5. Since you are a bit tight ... time, let's come ... the point.
6. You expressed interest ... a factory tour last time.
7. Well, I'm glad we could agree ... the new terms of payment and delivery.
8. We can continue our conversation ... lunch.
9. Should you come over to America again I would be pleased to welcome you ... Reebok International Ltd.
10. Thank you ... visiting our company.

UNIT 7   MAKING AN ENQUIRY

7.1 Key facts

In general, businessmen send <u>enquiries</u> to companies that supply goods asking for detailed information about their product range, or a price list, a catalogue, a <u>sample</u> or a <u>pattern</u>.

An enquiry usually involves the buyer asking for information on the following:

- Products (description, quality, material, <u>dimensions</u>, <u>features</u>, benefits, etc).
- Prices and discounts
- <u>Terms of payment</u>
- <u>Terms of delivery</u>
- <u>Delivery dates</u>

There is a general difference in meaning between samples and patterns.

Sample: a small amount of fabric, food, or other product, given to a prospective customer so that he can get an idea of what it is like; eg a free sample of shampoo in a magazine or a sachet of coffee at a trade fair.

Pattern: a small piece of material (cloth, wool, carpet, paper, etc) that shows what a larger piece (of the usual size) will look like. A pattern helps you choose the design of something.

7.2 Emails

7.2.1 Sportarena, Germany to Reebok, USA

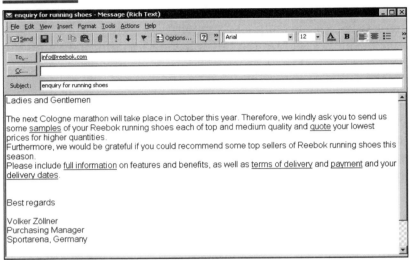

To... | info@reebok.com
Cc... |
Subject: | enquiry for running shoes

Ladies and Gentlemen

The next Cologne marathon will take place in October this year. Therefore, we kindly ask you to send us some samples of your Reebok running shoes each of top and medium quality and quote your lowest prices for higher quantities.
Furthermore, we would be grateful if you could recommend some top sellers of Reebok running shoes this season.
Please include full information on features and benefits, as well as terms of delivery and payment and your delivery dates.

Best regards

Volker Zöllner
Purchasing Manager
Sportarena, Germany

7.2.2 Broken English Berlin, Germany to Twinings, UK

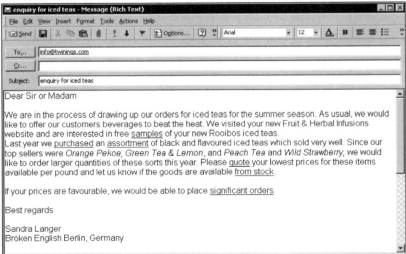

To... | info@twinings.com
Cc... |
Subject: | enquiry for iced teas

Dear Sir or Madam

We are in the process of drawing up our orders for iced teas for the summer season. As usual, we would like to offer our customers beverages to beat the heat. We visited your new Fruit & Herbal Infusions website and are interested in free samples of your new Rooibos iced teas.
Last year we purchased an assortment of black and flavoured iced teas which sold very well. Since our top sellers were *Orange Pekoe, Green Tea & Lemon,* and *Peach Tea* and *Wild Strawberry,* we would like to order larger quantities of these sorts this year. Please quote your lowest prices for these items available per pound and let us know if the goods are available from stock.

If your prices are favourable, we would be able to place significant orders.

Best regards

Sandra Langer
Broken English Berlin, Germany

7.3 Text components

ME1 We visited your website and have learned that you are among the TOP 10 manufacturers of sportswear. Please send us your latest catalogue and your price list.

> *Wir haben Ihre Website besucht und erfahren, dass Sie zu den führenden 10 Herstellern von Sportartikeln gehören. Bitte schicken Sie uns Ihren neuesten Katalog und Ihre Preisliste.*

ME2 We discovered on the Internet that you are one of the leading exporters of tea. We would be grateful if you could send us samples of your latest green teas. If the teas meet with our approval, we will be prepared to place a trial order.

> *Wir haben im Internet erfahren, dass Sie einer der führenden Tee-Exporteure sind. Über die Zusendung von Proben Ihrer neuesten Grüntees wären wir Ihnen dankbar. Wenn uns die Proben zusagen, sind wir gerne bereit, einen Probeauftrag zu erteilen.*

ME3 At the *ISPO* in Munich we met your Sales Manager, Mr Hallman, and learnt that you have launched a new running shoe. Please send us a quotation for this product including information on prices and quantity discounts, terms of payment and delivery as well as delivery dates.

> *Auf der ISPO in München haben wir Ihren Verkaufsleiter, Herrn Hallman kennen gelernt und erfahren, dass Sie einen neuen Laufschuh auf den Markt gebracht haben. Bitte machen Sie uns ein Angebot über diesen Artikel mit Angabe Ihrer Preise und Mengenrabatte, Zahlungs- und Lieferbedingungen sowie Liefertermine.*

ME4 Due to the Cologne marathon we have received many enquiries from customers for running shoes. Therefore, please let us know on what terms you can supply larger quantities of running shoes and if they are available from stock. We are convinced that good business could be developed, if your prices are favorable. **(AE)**

Aufgrund des Köln-Marathons haben wir viele Anfragen von Kunden über Laufschuhe erhalten. Bitte teilen Sie uns mit, zu welchen Bedingungen Sie größere Mengen dieser Artikel liefern können und ob Sie diese auf Lager haben. Wir sind überzeugt, dass sich gute Geschäfte entwickeln können, wenn Ihre Preise günstig sind.

ME5 Please send us your quotation and samples for *Durable Original 30* clip folders, in a range of colours and let us know how they are boxed. We have good contacts to government ministries and are convinced that your clip folders will sell well in Saudi Arabia, provided that your prices are competitive and your goods of supreme quality.

Bitte senden Sie uns ein Angebot und Muster Ihrer Klemmhefter Durable Original 30 in verschiedenen Farben und teilen Sie uns mit, wie diese verpackt sind. Wir verfügen über gute Kontakte zu Regierungsministerien und sind überzeugt, dass sich Ihre Klemmhefter in Saudi Arabien gut verkaufen lassen, vorausgesetzt Ihre Preise sind konkurrenzfähig und Ihre Produkte hochwertig.

ME6 Please quote for 5,000 *hp 945c* printers and send us a detailed product description. If your terms are favorable, we will place orders for higher quantities. **(AE)**

Bitte machen Sie uns ein Angebot über 5.000 Drucker hp 945c und senden Sie uns eine ausführliche Produktbeschreibung. Wenn Ihre Bedingungen günstig sind, werden wir Ihnen größere Aufträge zukommen lassen.

7.4 Tasks

Please make <u>enquiries</u> by email using the following details and make use of the text components wherever you can:

7.4.1 Saturn, Germany to Microsoft, USA

- Betreff/Anrede
- Sie machen eine Anfrage über Office Small Business Edition 2003 OEM[4]-Version und Office Edition 2003 für Schüler, Studenten und Lehrkräfte.
- Sie haben die Informationen zu den o.g. Produkten dem Internet entnommen.
- Sie planen eine Sonderaktion: Hardware + Software!
- Sie haben noch größere Restbestände an Rechnern verschiedener Anbieter auf Lager und wollen diese dem Endverbraucher zusammen mit der Software *Microsoft Office Small Business Edition 2003 OEM-Version* als Paket anbieten.
- Um vor der *CeBIT*[5] Mitte März zufriedenstellende Absätze erzielen zu können, bitten Sie um einen Sonderpreis für diese Aktion.
- Da Ihnen bekannt ist, dass Microsoft auf der *CeBIT* ihre neue *Office Small Business Edition 2005* vorzustellen wird, wäre das sicherlich eine gute Gelegenheit, um die Restbestände der Vorgänger-*Edition 2003* zu verkaufen.
- Sie wollen wissen, ob die *Office Edition 2003* für Schüler, Studenten und Lehrkräfte auf 2005 upgegradet werden kann.
- Sie bitten um Mitteilung der günstigsten Preise bei einer Mengenabnahme von je 1.000 Stück pro Artikel.
- Sie bitten um Angabe der Liefer– und Zahlungsbedingungen, sowie der Lieferzeiten.
- Schlusssatz

7.4.2 Office Supplies, Saudi Arabia to Durable, Germany

- Betreff/Anrede
- Sie machen eine Anfrage über Klemmhefter *Duraclip* und *Swingclip*.
- Sie stellen sich als einer der führenden Großhändler für Bürobedarf in Saudi Arabien mit besten Kontakten zu Regierungsministerien vor.

[4] OEM= Original Equipment Manufacturer, ie with hotline

[5] International trade fair for information technology, telecommunications, software & services

- Sie haben den Gebietsleiter für den Mittleren Osten von Durable, Herrn Berger, auf der Messe *Paperworld*[6] in Frankfurt kennen gelernt.
- Sie sind besonders an den Klemmheftern für den arabischen Markt interessiert, wo Sie große Absatzmöglichkeiten sehen.
- Muster der *Duraclips* haben Sie bereits auf der Messe erhalten. Sie bitten noch um Zusendung von Mustern der *Swingclips* 2260, 2266 und 2269 in verschiedenen Farben per Luftpost.
- Sie wollen sich von der guten Qualität der Produkte überzeugen und bitten um ein ausführliches Angebot mit Angabe der äußersten Preise sowie der Zahlungs- und Lieferbedingungen.
- Wenn die Preise konkurrenzfähig sind, wären Sie bereit, einen Probeauftrag zu erteilen.
- Schlusssatz

7.4.3 Fill in the missing prepositions

1. Dear Sir ... Madam
2. We have seen your advertisement ... the Internet and noted that you have launched a new running shoe, especially suited for marathons, ... the market.
3. Please quote ... 500 items of this model.
4. There is a considerable demand ... these running shoes ... this market, and we are convinced that the goods will sell well.
5. During a visit ... the *ISPO* in Munich ... the beginning of February, we saw your new design ... soccer shoes ... adults and kids which should also be of interest ... our customers.
6. Please let us know ... what terms and ... what prices you can supply these soccer shoes.
7. Your prompt quotation ... email would be appreciated.
8. Please send a sample of this soccer shoe ... courier service.
9. If your sample shoes meet ... our approval, we would be prepared to place a trial order.
10. Additionally, we would like to know whether you could supply ... stock?

---

[6] International trade fair for office equipment

UNIT 8   SUBMITTING AN OFFER

8.1 Key facts

After receiving an enquiry the seller has to <u>submit</u> an offer or a <u>quotation</u>. If requested by the enquirer, <u>samples</u> or <u>patterns</u> have to be send along with the quotation as an enclosure or may be sent <u>under separate cover</u>.

An offer or a quotation should include the following details:

- Description of the goods
- Quantity
- Prices and possible discounts
- Delivery dates
- Terms of delivery
- Terms of payment

8.2 Letters
8.2.1 Reebok, USA to Sportarena, Germany

Reebok International Ltd
1895 J W Foster Boulevard   Canton, MA 02021   USA
Phone: 1-800-934-3566   Fax: 1-800-934-3455
Internet: www.reebok.com

TH/pj

March 23, 2005

Sportarena
z. Hd. Volker Zoellner
Neumarkt 10
50969 Koeln
Germany

Quotation for running shoes

Dear Mr Zoellner

In reply to your email dated March 21, we have pleasure in enclosing a sample of our top quality product, our *Reebok Premier Ultra DMX Running Shoe Mens*, item 1388742, which may be of interest to you. This item is also available for women. Today's price for this item for men or women is US$109.99, availability: in stock.

The <u>features</u> and benefits are as follows:

Features	Benefits
Midsole Material: Compression Molded EVA	The EVA material is heated, reducing the density, thereby making it lighter.
Cushioning Technology: DMX Foam	DMX foam offers comfortable cushioning.
Heel Technology: DMX Shear	A heel cushioning, footstrike management system, which helps reduce impact on strike.
Outsole: Carbon Rubber	Carbon rubber outsole provides durability and traction.

For further information please visit our website <u>www.store.reebok.com</u>.

Additionally, we enclose a sample of our classic running shoe, *Reebok Premier Road Plus Running Shoe Womens*, item 1328541, which we offer for both men and women at a price of US$79.99 for immediate delivery.

Furthermore, we would like to draw your attention to our latest top seller:
Reebok circa Casual Shoe Mens or Womens, item no 1427401, at a price of US$69.99 per item.

As you will see from our sample shoe enclosed, this running shoe is stylish and comfortable and can be worn as a casual shoe or for running. The padded foam sockliner and molded midsole provide cushioning, comfort and durability, while the perforated leather upper offers breathability and comfort.

We have a limited number of pieces of each size available for immediate delivery. All items are available <u>subject to prior sale</u>.

Prices: Our prices are quoted CIF Hamburg.
           We will grant a <u>special discount</u> of 20% on our list prices on all orders <u>exceeding</u> US$10,000.

Payment: <u>Letter of Credit</u> opened in our favor at the Bank of America, Boston, USA only.

We hope that our samples <u>will meet with your approval</u> and we look forward to hearing from you soon.

Sincerely

Reebok International Ltd, USA
Tony Hancock
Tony Hancock
Sales Manger

Enc

8.2.2 Twinings, UK to Broken English Berlin, Germany

TWININGS
OF LONDON

South Way   Andover Hampshire   SP105AQ   Great Britain
Telephone: + 44 (0) 1264 334477 Fax: + 44 (0) 1264 335577
Internet: www.twinings.com

JR

2 February 2005

Ms Sandra Langer
Broken English
Koertestrasse 10
10967 Berlin
Germany

Dear Ms Langer

Quotation for iced teas

We thank you for your email of today and are pleased to <u>submit</u> the following quotation:

Orange Pekoe, TOP 124	£15.95 per lb[7]
Green Tea & Lemon	£14.95 per lb
Peach Tea	£14.95 per lb
Wild Strawberry	£11.00 per lb

Prices: all orders <u>exceeding</u> £ 3,000 less 15%
<u>Terms of payment</u>: 30 days net, 14 days 2%
Delivery: <u>from stock</u>, DDU

We learned from your email that you are also interested in our Rooibos teas. As requested please find enclosed a choice of our favourite sorts
Strawberry cream
Strawberry, orange and yoghurt
Strawberry and kiwi
which we can offer at a price of £9.95 per lb.

We hope that you will enjoy the sample of our tea of the month: *Green Tea & Mandarin* at a price of £14.95 per lb.

---

[7] 1 pound (lb) = 453,59 g

For further information please visit our website www.twinings.com to discover our full range of finest and speciality teas.

We hope that our offer meets with your approval. We look forward to hearing from you soon and receiving your first order, which we will process with utmost priority.

Yours sincerely

Janet Read

Janet Read
Sales Director

Enclosures

8.3 Text components

SO1 Thank you for your enquiry of today for 1,000 *hp nc4000 Notebook PCs*. We are glad to offer as follows: …

Attached please find a detailed product description as a PDF file. Should you be interested in a demonstration on your premises, please let us know.

> *Wir danken für Ihre Anfrage von heute über 1.000 hp Notebook PCs nc4000 und bieten wie folgt an: ...*
>
> *Anbei finden Sie eine detaillierte Produktbeschreibung als PDF-Datei. Sollten Sie an einer Vorführung in Ihrem Hause interessiert sein, so teilen Sie uns das bitte mit.*

SO2 We thank you for your enquiry of May 22, 2005 and are glad to inform you that sample shoes of our latest *Reebok Premier Road Plus Running Shoe*, item 1328541, have been rushed to you today by courier service.

We quote as follows:

Prices: FOB Hamburg, list prices less 15% trade discount

Delivery: from stock, while stocks last

Payment: 30 days net, 14 days 2%

This offer is valid for two weeks. **(AE)**

> *Wir danken Ihnen für Ihre Anfrage vom 22. Mai 2005 und freuen uns, Ihnen mitzuteilen, dass Musterschuhe*

unseres neuesten Laufschuhs Reebok Premier Road Plus Running Shoe, Artikel-Nr. 1328541, heute per Kurierdienst an Sie versandt wurden.
Wir bieten wie folgt an:
Preise: *FOB Hamburg, Listenpreise ./. 15% Händlerrabatt*
Lieferung: *ab Lager, solange der Vorrat reicht*
Zahlung: *30 Tage 2%, 14 Tage netto*
Das Angebot ist 2 Wochen gültig.

SO3 Thank you for your enquiry of today for plastic folders. We are glad to quote as follows:
Prices: CIF Djidda, Saudi Arabia, catalogue prices less 10% discount for orders received before 1 January 2005
Payment: L/C
Delivery: immediately after opening of L/C
> *Wir danken Ihnen für Ihre heutige Anfrage über Schnellhefter und unterbreiten Ihnen folgendes Angebot:*
> ***Preise:*** *CIF Djidda, Saudi Arabien, 10% Rabatt auf unsere Katalogpreise bei Auftragserteilung bis zum 1. Januar 2005*
> ***Zahlung:*** *Dokumenten-Akkreditiv*
> ***Lieferung:*** *sofort nach Akkreditiv-Eröffnung*

SO4 We thank you for your enquiry of today for transparent pockets and are glad to submit you the following quotation:
Prices: C+F New York, catalogue prices less 10% discount for quantities exceeding 100,000 items
Delivery: within 2 weeks after receipt of order
Payment: by SWIFT after receipt of invoice
This offer is valid for three weeks.
Since we have not done business with you before, please let us have your trade references when placing your order.

Wir danken Ihnen für Ihre heutige Anfrage über Klarsichthüllen und freuen uns, Ihnen folgendes Angebot zu unterbreiten:
Preise: *C+F New York, Katalogpreise ./. 10% Mengenrabatt bei Abnahmemengen ab 100.000 Stück*
Lieferung: *innerhalb von 2 Wochen nach Auftragserhalt*
Zahlung: *per SWIFT nach Erhalt der Rechnung*
Das Angebot ist drei Wochen gültig.
Da wir Sie als Geschäftspartner noch nicht kennen, bitten wir bei Auftragserteilung um Angabe Ihrer Handelsreferenzen.

SO5 For popular downloads, please visit our website at www.microsoft.com.
Should you require any further information, please do not hesitate to contact us.

Beliebte Downloads finden Sie auf unserer Website www.microsoft.com.
Sollten Sie noch weitere Informationen benötigen, so teilen Sie uns das bitte mit.

SO6 Subject to our General Terms and Conditions which are available at www.hp.com

Es gelten unsere Allgemeinen Geschäftsbedingungen, die Sie auf unserer Website www.hp.com finden.

8.4 Incoterms (International Commercial Terms) 2000

Incoterms make international trade easier and help traders in different countries to understand one another. Essentially, these standardised delivery terms <u>govern</u> where the goods are <u>picked up</u> by (or are delivered to) the buyer, who is responsible for insuring the goods <u>in transit</u> and for bearing the risk of the <u>shipment</u>, and who pays the custom's duties. Incoterms were developed by the <u>International Chamber of Commerce</u> in Paris, and are most commonly used in international contracts as follows:

Incoterms 2000	Meaning in English	Meaning in German
	All modes of transport including multimodal transport	**Alle Transportarten, einschließlich multimodaler Transport**
EXW	Ex Works … (named place)	Ab Werk … (benannter Ort)
FCA	Free Carrier …(named place)	Frei Frachtführer … (benannter Ort)
CPT	Carriage Paid To … (named place of destination)	Frachtfrei … (benannter Bestimmungsort)
CIP	Carriage and Insurance Paid to … (named place of destination)	Frachtfrei versichert … (benannter Bestimmungsort)
DAF	Delivered At Frontier … (named place)	Geliefert Grenze … (benannter Ort)
DDU	Delivery Duty Unpaid … (named place)	Geliefert unverzollt … (benannter Ort)
DDP	Delivery Duty Paid … (named place)	Geliefert verzollt (benannter Ort)
	Transport by air or rail	**Luft- und Eisenbahntransport**
FCA	Free Carrier … (named place)	Frei Frachtführer … (benannter Ort)
	Transport by sea	**Seetransport**
FAS	Free Alongside Ship … (named port of shipment)	Frei Längsseite Schiff … (Benannter Verschiffungshafen)
FOB	Free On Board … (named port of shipment)	Frei an Bord … (benannter Verschiffungshafen)
CFR	Cost and Freight … (named port of destination)	Kosten und Fracht (benannter Bestimmungshafen)
CIF	Cost, Insurance, Freight … (named port of destination)	Kosten, Versicherung, Fracht (benannter Bestimmungshafen)
DES	Delivered EX Ship … (named port of destination)	Geliefert ab Schiff … (benannter Bestimmungshafen)
DEQ	Delivered Ex Quay … (duty paid) (named port of destination)	Geliefert ab Kai (verzollt) (benannter Bestimmungshafen)

Incoterms 2000 only apply when <u>incorporated</u> into the contract of sale.

8.4.1 Overview Incoterms 2000

	INCO TERMS 2000	Contract of transport	Customs clearance for exportation	Customs clearance for importation	Transport insurance*	Risk transfer from seller to buyer	Cost transfer
Group E minimum risk for seller	EXW	buyer	buyer	buyer	buyer	named place of seller's works	named place of seller's works
	FCA	buyer	seller	buyer	buyer	place of handing over to first carrier	place of handing over to first carrier
Group F seller does not pay <u>main carriage</u>	FAS	buyer	seller	buyer	buyer	alongside ship at the <u>port of shipment</u>	alongside ship at the port of shipment
	FOB	buyer	seller	buyer	buyer	<u>ship's rail</u> at the port of shipment	ship's rail at the port of shipment
	CFR	seller	seller	buyer	buyer	ship's rail at the port of shipment	named <u>port of destination</u>
Group C seller pays main carriage	CIF	seller	seller	buyer	seller (minimum cover)	ship's rail at the port of shipment	named port of destination
	CPT	Seller	seller	buyer	buyer	place of handing over to first carrier	named place of destination
	CIP	seller	seller	buyer	seller (minimum cover)	place of handing over to first carrier	named place of destination
	DAF	seller	seller	buyer	buyer	named place at frontier	named place at frontier
	DES	seller	seller	buyer	buyer	named port of destination	named port of destination
Group D maximum risk for seller	DEQ	seller	seller	buyer	buyer	quay at the port of destination	quay at the port of destination
	DDU	seller	seller	buyer	buyer	named place of destination	named place of destination
	DDP	seller	seller	seller	buyer	named place of destination	named place of destination

NB: <u>At any rate</u>, the transport insurance should be agreed upon, even in the case of **CIF** and **CIP,** as the seller is required to obtain insurance only on minimum cover. Should the buyer wish to have the protection of greater cover, he would either need to agree as much expressly with the seller or to make his own extra insurance arrangements.

More information on Incoterms will be found at <u>www.iccwbo.org/ index_incoterms.asp</u>.

8.5 <u>Terms of payment</u> in foreign trade

The terms of payment in foreign trade regulate the conditions under which the buyer is to <u>effect payment</u>. Conditions range from short-term to medium-term or long-term.

ENGLISH	GERMAN
Short-term conditions	**Kurzfristige Zahlungsbedingungen**
Payment in advance	Vorauszahlung
Cash upfront	Barzahlung im Voraus
Cash with order	Barzahlung bei Auftragserteilung
14 days 2%, 30 days net (2/14, net 30)	Zahlung innerhalb von 14 Tagen abzüglich 2% Skonto oder innerhalb von 30 Tagen netto
Cash against documents	Kasse gegen Dokumente
Documents against acceptance	Auslieferung der Dokumente gegen Akzept
Payment by irrevocable and confirmed documentary letter of credit	Zahlung durch unwiderrufliches und bestätigtes Dokumentenakkreditiv
Payment by SWIFT	Zahlung per SWIFT
Payment by crossed cheque	Zahlung per Verrechnungsscheck
Medium-term conditions	**Mittelfristige Zahlungsbedingungen**
Payment within 60/90 days from date of invoice	Zahlung innerhalb von 60/90 Tagen nach Rechnungsdatum
1/3 with order, 1/3 on delivery, and 1/3 two months after delivery	1/3 bei Auftragserteilung, 1/3 bei Lieferung und 1/3 innerhalb von 2 Monaten nach Lieferung
Long-term conditions	**Langfristige Zahlungsbedingungen**
20% when placing the order, 20% on delivery, 60% by 3 instalments, commencing 2 months after delivery	20% bei Auftragserteilung, 20% bei Lieferung, 60% in 3 Ratenzahlungen beginnend 2 Monate nach Lieferung

8.5.1 Overview payment in foreign trade

Method of payment	Settlement	Reasons
Payment in advance	The buyer pays the full purchase price to the seller before shipment is made.	The customer is still unknown and has no credit history.
Letter of Credit L/C	It is an obligation by a bank to effect payment by order of an importer to conditions exactly stipulated on presentation of agreed and proper documents.	The customer is still unknown and has no credit history. **or** The customer is known but there is uncertainty about his solvency.
Cash against documents CAD	The importer receives the documents on payment of the equivalent sum of money.	The customer is known but there is uncertainty about his solvency.
Documents against acceptance D/A	The buyer is delivered the agreed documents only by accepting a draft presented by a bank on behalf of the exporter.	The customer is known, however, he needs a credit period. There is uncertainty about his solvency. A bank provides security.
Payment on receipt of goods	On release of the agreed documents to the importer, he takes possession of the goods. The exporter has no assurance that payment will be effected after receipt of the goods.	Common terms of payment for EC, EFTA and the other western industrial countries where customers are known and secure. No bank is involved.
Payment by SWIFT	The bank-to-bank segment of SWIFT settles payment of the invoice after receipt of goods.	The customer is known. The commercial value of the goods varies.

Method of payment	Settlement	Reasons
Payment by <u>crossed</u> <u>cheque</u>	Payment of the invoice is settled by bank-to-bank drawing after receipt of the goods. The importer <u>draws a</u> <u>cheque</u> on the exporter's bank and sends it to the exporter. The exporter presents this cheque to his bankers who will <u>credit</u> the equivalent to his <u>account</u>.	Preferred by Anglo-American customers. Generally, the commercial value of the goods <u>exceeds</u> € 1,000.

8.5.2 SWIFT (Society for Worldwide Interbank Financial Telecommunication)

was created in the 1970s to meet the need of the banks to settle the growing number of cross-border payments. Over the last three decades, this has grown into a business of routinely 7 million messages per day. <u>Bulk payment transfer messages</u> allow <u>batching</u> an unlimited number of payment instructions in an electronic file. For more information please visit <u>www.swift.com</u>

8.5.3 Letter of Credit (L/C)

A letter of credit can be regarded as the safest <u>means of payment</u> in foreign trade because of the following <u>features</u>:

- Payment of the documents' equivalent is guaranteed by a bank.
- <u>Insolvency</u> of a buyer is <u>safeguarded.</u>
- Procedure is <u>subject to</u> the uniform <u>regulations</u> of the <u>International Chamber of Commerce</u> in Paris.
- All parties deal with documents rather than goods.
- Banks are not responsible for the <u>genuineness</u>, form or <u>legal</u> <u>effect</u> of the documents.

8.5.3.1 Types of L/C:

<u>Revocable</u> **L/C:** can be <u>modified</u> or <u>annulled</u> at any time by the importer **without** the consent of all parties.

<u>Irrevocable</u> **L/C:** can only be modified or annulled **with** the consent of all parties.

Confirmed L/C: In addition to the bank of the importer, the bank of the exporter confirms the credit. Thus both banks are <u>liable for</u> the payment of the documents. (A confirmed L/C is advisable because owing to political or economic events in the importing country payment of the documents' equivalent might be questioned if under certain conditions, the importing bank cannot provide adequate cover or if the central bank does not provide the necessary foreign currency.)

Irrevocable and confirmed L/C: provides maximum security.

8.5.3.2 Procedure of payment by irrevocable and confirmed documentary Letter of Credit

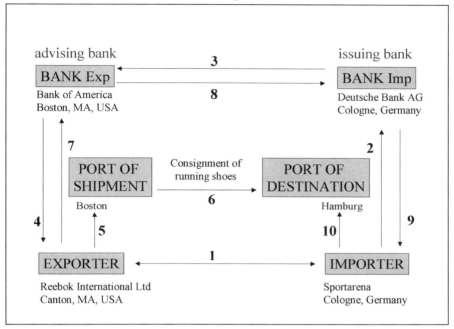

The exporter (*Reebok International Ltd, USA*) and the importer (*Sportarena, Köln*) agree on

Step 1 Payment of the goods (eg running shoes) by irrevocable and confirmed <u>Letter of Credit</u>.

Step 2 The importer (*Sportarena, Köln*) arranges with his bank (*Deutsche Bank AG, Köln*) for the <u>issuance of L/C </u>in the exporter's favour (*Reebok International Ltd, USA*).

Step 3 The issuing bank (*Deutsche Bank AG, Köln*) opens the credit and sends copies of the L/C to the advising bank (*Bank of America, Boston, USA*).

Step 4 The advising bank (*Bank of America, Boston, USA*) sends a copy of the L/C to the exporter's credit department (*Reebok International Ltd, USA*).

Step 5 The exporter (*Reebok International Ltd, USA*) arranges shipment of the goods *(eg running shoes)* and receives the shipping papers (eg B/L, commercial invoice in duplicate, packing list, insurance policy).

Step 6 The goods *(eg running shoes)* are on their way from the port of shipment (Boston) to the agreed port of destination (Hamburg).

Step 7 The exporter (*Reebok International Ltd, USA*) sends all the documentation required in the L/C (eg B/L, commercial invoice in duplicate, packing list, insurance policy) along with a draft for payment to his bank *(Bank of America, Boston, USA)* via express courier.

Step 8 The advising bank *(Bank of America, Boston, USA)* reviews all documentation to ensure it complies with the L/C. After review of the documentation, it credits the exporter's account (*Reebok International Ltd, USA*) with the amount of the L/C minus applicable fees and forwards the documentation to the issuing bank (*Deutsche Bank AG, Köln*).

Step 9 On receipt of the documentation, the issuing bank (*Deutsche Bank AG, Köln*) honours the L/C and debits the importer's account (*Sportarena, Köln*) with the amount of the credit minus applicable fees. The issuing bank (*Deutsche Bank AG, Köln*) forwards the funds to the advising bank *(Bank of America, Boston, USA)* and sends the documentation to the importer (*Sportarena, Köln*).

Step 10 On presentation of the documentation (eg B/L, commercial invoice in duplicate, packing list, insurance policy), the importer (*Sportarena, Köln*) receives the goods from the shipping company and the customs in the agreed port of destination (Hamburg).

8.6 Tasks

Please <u>submit</u> offers by email using the following details and make use of the text components wherever you can:

8.6.1 Microsoft, USA to Saturn, Germany

- Anrede/Betreff
- Sie danken für die Anfrage über *Office Small Business Edition 2003 OEM-Version* und *Office Edition 2003 für Schüler, Studenten und Lehrkräfte.*
- Da Sie vor der *CeBIT* viele Anfragen von Kunden zu den o.g. Artikeln erhalten haben, bieten Sie folgende Sonderpreise an: *Office Small Business Edition 2003 OEM* bei Mengenabnahmen bis 1.000 Stück zu US$ 119,-; ab 1.000 Stück zu US$ 100,- pro Stück.
- Preis: *Office Edition 2003 für Schüler, Studenten und Lehrkräfte* bis 1.000 Stück zu US$ 139,-; ab 1.000 Stück zu US$ 119,-.
- Preise: CIF Hamburg; auf Wunsch kann Versand per Luftfracht vereinbart werden.
- Zahlung: Kasse gegen Dokumente.
- Lieferzeit: ca. 8-10 Tage nach Auftragseingang.
- Weitere Informationen zu Upgrades auf *Office 2005* und weiteren Editionen sowie Editionen im Vergleich finden Sie unter <u>www.microsoft.com</u>.
- Sie weisen auf die *Microsoft TOU (Terms of Use)* hin, die ebenfalls auf der Website erläutert sind.
- Für eventuelle Rückfragen stehen Sie gerne zur Verfügung.
- Schlusssatz

8.6.2 Durable, Germany to Office Supplies, Saudi Arabia

- Anrede/Betreff
- Sie danken für die Anfrage und das Interesse an den Klemmheftern für den arabischen Markt.
- Die Muster der *Swingclips* 2260, 2266 und 2269 sind heute per Kurierdienst verschickt worden.
- Falls der Kunde noch keinen Katalog auf der Messe bekommen hat, senden Sie zusammen mit der Mustersendung den neuesten Katalog über alle Durable-Neuheiten.
- Als Dateianhang senden Sie eine Produktbeschreibung der Artikel

  a) Klemmappe *Duraclip Original 30* mit transparentem Vorderdeckel in 12 Farben. Fassungsvermögen: 1-30 Blatt DIN A4; Verpackung: 25 Stück im Karton; Preis: € 1,00 pro Stück FOB.

  b) Klemmappe *Swingclip* mit transparenter, flexibler Hartfolie. Fassungsvermögen:
  1-30 Blatt DIN A4; Verpackung: 25 Stück im Karton; Preis: € 1,00 pro Stück FOB.
- Mindestauftragswert € 5.000,-. Ab einem Auftragswert von € 10.000,- kann ein Mengenrabatt von 10% auf die Listenpreise gewährt werden.
- Preise: FOB Hamburg + Verschiffungskosten = C+F Djidda, Saudi Arabien.
- Lieferung: Ware ist auf Lager.
- Zahlung: Da Sie den Kunden als Geschäftspartner noch nicht kennen, bitten Sie beim Erstauftrag um Zahlung per L/C, bei Folgeaufträgen kann die Zahlung CAD erfolgen.
- Weitere Informationen über Ihre Produkte sowie Ihre Allgemeinen Geschäftsbedingungen sind unter www.durable.de zu finden.
- Für eventuelle Rückfragen stehen Sie gerne zur Verfügung.
- Schlusssatz

8.6.3 Fill in the missing prepositions

1. Thank you … your enquiry … March 1, 2005 … 2,000 *hp 234c* flat screens.
2. The flat screens can be delivered immediately … receipt … your order.
3. Delivery cannot be promised … 2 months … we receive your order … the end of March.
4. Payment … 60 days … date of invoice.
5. Payment … irrevocable and confirmed L/C.
6. This offer is valid … 3 weeks.
7. We assure you that your order will be executed … your complete satisfaction.
8. You may rely … the prompt and careful execution … your order.
9. Subject … our General Terms and Conditions which are availabe … www.hp.com .
10. One-third … order, one-third … delivery, and one-third … 30 days … delivery.

UNIT 9   PLACING AN ORDER

9.1 Key facts

If the buyer is interested in the seller's goods and accepts the conditions of his offer, he will place an order. If the buyer does not agree to the terms and conditions of a previous offer, he usually tries to negotiate the terms by submitting a counter offer.

9.2 Emails

9.2.1 Sportarena, Germany to Reebok, USA

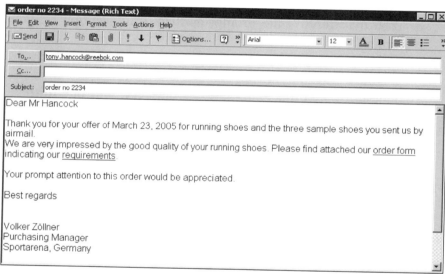

ORDER FORM No 1234   Date: March 26, 2005

Quantity	Item	Size	Unit Price in US$	Amount in US$
20	1388742 *Reebok Premier Ultra DMX Running Shoe Men*	42	109.99	2,199.80
20	ditto	43	109.99	2,199.80
20	ditto	44	109.99	2,199.80
10	ditto	45	109.99	1,099.90
10	1388741 *Reebok Premier Ultra DMX Running Shoe Women*	37	109.99	1,099.90
20	ditto	38	109.99	2,199.80

Quantity	Item	Size	Unit Price in US$	Amount in US$
20	ditto	39	109.99	2,199.80
20	ditto	40	109.99	2,199.80
10	ditto	41	109.99	1,099.90
20	1328542 *Reebok Premier Road Plus Running Shoe Men*	42	79,99	1,599.80
20	ditto	43	79.99	1,599.80
20	ditto	44	79.99	1,599.80
10	ditto	45	79.99	799.90
10	1328541 *Reebok Premier Road Plus Running Shoe Women*	37	79.99	799.90
20	ditto	38	79.99	1,599.80
20	ditto	39	79.99	1,599.80
20	ditto	40	79.99	1,599.80
10	ditto	41	79.99	799.90
20	1427402 *Reebok circa Casual Shoe Men*	42	69.99	1,399.80
20	ditto	43	69.99	1,399.80
20	ditto	44	69.99	1,399.80
10	ditto	45	69.99	699.90
10	1427401 *Reebok circa Casual Shoe Women*	37	69.99	699.90
20	ditto	38	69.99	1,399.80
20	ditto	39	69.99	1,399.80
20	ditto	40	69.99	1,399.80
10	ditto	41	69.99	699.90
			total	US$38,995.50
			./. 20% special discount	US$7,799.10
			total amount FOB	**US$31,196.40**
			+ **freight**	**US$3,000.00**
			+ insurance	**US$200.00**
			total value CIF Hamburg	**US$34,396.40**

Prices: CIF Hamburg
Payment: L/C
Delivery: after receipt of notification on opening of L/C

The delivery date on our order form must be observed and the goods must be in conformity with the sample shoes. Please note that we must hold you responsible for all losses arising from any delay in delivery.
Shipping marks will follow.

9.2.2 Broken English Berlin, Germany to Twinings, UK

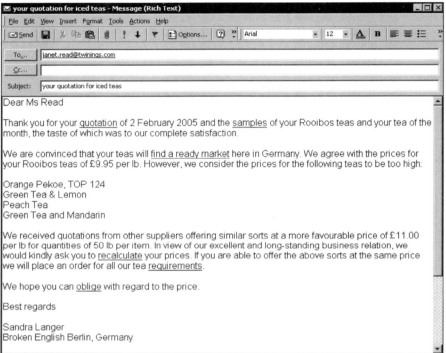

Dear Ms Read

Thank you for your quotation of 2 February 2005 and the samples of your Rooibos teas and your tea of the month, the taste of which was to our complete satisfaction.

We are convinced that your teas will find a ready market here in Germany. We agree with the prices for your Rooibos teas of £9.95 per lb. However, we consider the prices for the following teas to be too high:

Orange Pekoe, TOP 124
Green Tea & Lemon
Peach Tea
Green Tea and Mandarin

We received quotations from other suppliers offering similar sorts at a more favourable price of £11.00 per lb for quantities of 50 lb per item. In view of our excellent and long-standing business relation, we would kindly ask you to recalculate your prices. If you are able to offer the above sorts at the same price we will place an order for all our tea requirements.

We hope you can oblige with regard to the price.

Best regards

Sandra Langer
Broken English Berlin, Germany

9.3 Text components

PO1   Thank you for your quotation of November 1, 2005 for running shoes. Please find attached our order for immediate delivery. Since we are in urgent need of the goods, please proceed our order with utmost priority.

The running shoes must correspond to the sample shoes. Running shoes of poor quality will be returned at your expense. **(AE)**

> *Danke für Ihr Angebot vom 1. November 2005 über Laufschuhe. Bitte merken Sie den Auftrag, den wir als Datei anhängen, zur sofortigen Lieferung vor. Da wir die Waren dringend benötigen, bitten wir Sie, unseren Auftrag mit höchster Priorität zu behandeln.*

Die Laufschuhe müssen den Musterschuhen entsprechen. Laufschuhe schlechter Qualität werden auf Ihre Kosten zurückgeschickt.

PO2 Attached please find our order form no 1234. The delivery date in our above order must be observed. Otherwise, we must hold you responsible for all loss resulting from any delay in delivery.

If this first order is carried out to our complete satisfaction, we are prepared to do regular business with you.

Als Dateianhang schicken wir Ihnen unser Auftragsformular Nr. 1234. Der Liefertermin in unserem o.g. Auftrag muss eingehalten werden. Andernfalls müssen wir Sie für jegliche Verluste, die bei einer Lieferverzögerung entstehen, verantwortlich machen.

Wenn dieser Erstauftrag zufriedenstellend ausgeführt wird, sind wir bereit, regelmäßige Geschäfte mit Ihnen zu tätigen.

PO3 We thank you for your quotation for iced teas and attach our order no 2234.

Your usual prompt attention to this order would be appreciated.

Wir danken Ihnen für Ihr Angebot über Eistees und senden Ihnen als Dateianhang unsere Bestellung Nr. 2234.

Wir hoffen, dass Sie diesen Auftrag wie immer pünktlich erledigen werden.

PO4 The flat screens must be delivered without fail by the end of November 2005 for our Christmas special. We reserve the right to cancel our order, if delivery is not effected by that date.

Please ensure appropriate packaging. Shipping marks will follow.

Die Flachbildschirme müssen unbedingt bis Ende November 2005 für unsere Weihnachtsaktion geliefert werden. Wir behalten uns das Recht vor, unseren Auftrag zu stornieren, wenn die Lieferung nicht bis zu diesem Termin erfolgt ist.
Bitte sorgen Sie für entsprechende Verpackung. Versandmarkierungen teilen wir Ihnen noch mit.

PO5 Unfortunately, we have to cancel our order no 3375 of 30 April 2005 for flat screens due to the bankruptcy of our key customer. We are very sorry for any inconvenience caused and hope to be able to make good for it soon.

Leider müssen wir unseren Auftrag Nr. 3375 vom 30. April 2005 über Flachbildschirme aufgrund des Konkurses unseres Hauptabnehmers stornieren. Wie bedauern die Ihnen entstandenen Unannehmlichkeiten sehr und hoffen, Sie bald entschädigen zu können.

9.4 Tasks

Please place orders by email using the following details and make use of the text components wherever you can:

9.4.1 Saturn, Germany to Microsoft Corp, USA

- Anrede/Betreff
- Sie danken für das Angebot vom … über *Office Small Business Edition 2003 OEM-Version* und *Office Edition 2003 für Schüler, Studenten und Lehrkräfte.*
- Der Preis für die *Office Small Business Edition 2003 OEM* von US$ 119,- bis 1.000 Stück erscheint Ihnen aber zu hoch und soll geprüft werden.
- Für das Geschäft vor der *CeBIT* wird eine Mengenabnahme von 1.000 Stück *Office Small Business Edition 2003 OEM-Version* in Aussicht gestellt, wenn eine Preisreduzierung von 15% auf diesen Artikel gewährt werden kann.
- Der Preis für die *Office Edition 2003 für Schüler, Studenten und Lehrkräfte* ist akzeptabel.

- Lieferung: CIP Flughafen Köln/Bonn.
- Versand: per Luftfracht.
- Zahlung: Kasse gegen Dokumente.
- Liefertermin: 8-10 Tage nach Auftragseingang.
- Als Handelsreferenz nennen Sie Apple Inc., USA, mit der Sie seit ca. 10 Jahren in Geschäftsverbindung stehen.
- Schlusssatz

9.4.2 Office Supplies, Saudi Arabia to Durable, Germany

- Anrede/Betreff
- Sie danken für das Angebot vom ... über Klemmhefter und die Mustersendung, die inzwischen eingegangen ist.
- Sie erteilen zunächst einen Probeauftrag, um zu sehen, wie sich die Ware auf dem arabischen Markt verkauft.
- Sie bestellen:

  a) 6.000 Klemmappe *Duraclip Original 30* mit transparentem Vorderdeckel in 12 Farben sortiert, d.h. 500 Stück pro Farbe. Fassungsvermögen: 1-30 Blatt DIN A4; Verpackung: 25 Stück im Karton; Preis: € 1,00 pro Stück FOB.

  b) 6.000 Klemmappe *Swingclip* mit transparenter, flexibler Hartfolie in 6 Farben. Fassungsvermögen: 1-30 Blatt DIN A4; Verpackung: 25 Stück im Karton; Preis: € 1,00 pro Stück FOB plus Frachtkosten.
- Preise: C+F Djidda, Saudi Arabien.
- Liefertermin: nach L/C-Eröffnung.
- Zahlung: L/C.
- Sie bitten um schnelle Zusendung einer Proforma-Rechnung zur L/C-Eröffnung.
- Schlusssatz

9.4.3 Fill in the missing prepositions

1. Thank you ... your quotation ... March 3, 2005 ... 1,000 *hp 945c* printers.
2. Please book the following order ... immediate delivery.
3. The goods must be delivered ... fail ... the end of October 2005.
4. Please see that the *hp 945c* printers are shipped ... the next vessel.
5. The delivery date ... 1 November 2005 must be strictly observed.
6. We must hold you responsible ... all losses resulting... any delay ... delivery.
7. The running shoes must correspond ... the samples.
8. Running shoes ... minor quality will be returned ... your expense.
9. Our offer is subject ... our General Terms and Conditions specified ... our website.
10. We are very sorry ... any inconvenience caused and hope to be able to make good ... it soon.

UNIT 10 OBTAINING CREDIT INFORMATION

10.1 Key facts

How do sellers know whom they can trust? In order to prevent a seller becoming endangered by financially weak or insolvent business partners he needs the following information about the buyer **before** executing his order:

- Financial standing
- Payment behaviour
- Turnover or sales effected in the previous year
- Credit limit

Reliable information on companies can be obtained from the following sources:

- Trade references given by the buyer
- Online information; eg buyer's balance sheet
- Bank references of the buyer
- Credit agencies

10.2 Credit Ageny

A credit agency is a company that collects information about the creditworthiness of individuals and corporations and provides it for a fee to interested parties.

Some agencies offer secure email support, ie you can safely exchange sensitive and confidential information whilst excluding unauthorized persons from reading the contents.

10.3 Export Credit Insurance

Since trading on credit terms has its risks (customer insolvency, commercial risks, political risks, overdue accounts, bad debt) export credit insurance policies are offered eg by EULER HERMES, a company belonging to the ALLIANZ GROUP and the leading credit insurer in Germany and the UK with subsidiaries all over the world. For more information please visit www.eulerhermes.com.

10.4 Emails
10.4.1 Reebok, USA to NIKE, USA

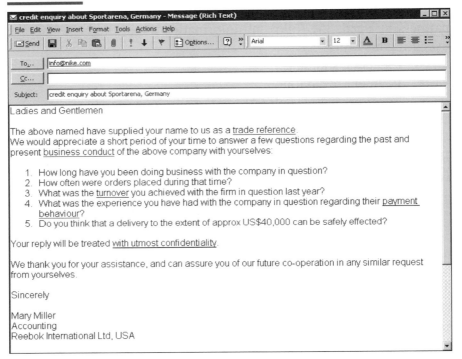

credit enquiry about Sportarena, Germany - Message (Rich Text)

File Edit View Insert Format Tools Actions Help

Send | Options... | Arial | 12 | **B**

To... | info@nike.com

Cc...

Subject: | credit enquiry about Sportarena, Germany

Ladies and Gentlemen

The above named have supplied your name to us as a trade reference.
We would appreciate a short period of your time to answer a few questions regarding the past and present business conduct of the above company with yourselves:

1. How long have you been doing business with the company in question?
2. How often were orders placed during that time?
3. What was the turnover you achieved with the firm in question last year?
4. What was the experience you have had with the company in question regarding their payment behaviour?
5. Do you think that a delivery to the extent of approx US$40,000 can be safely effected?

Your reply will be treated with utmost confidentiality.

We thank you for your assistance, and can assure you of our future co-operation in any similar request from yourselves.

Sincerely

Mary Miller
Accounting
Reebok International Ltd, USA

10.4.2 NIKE, USA to Reebok, USA

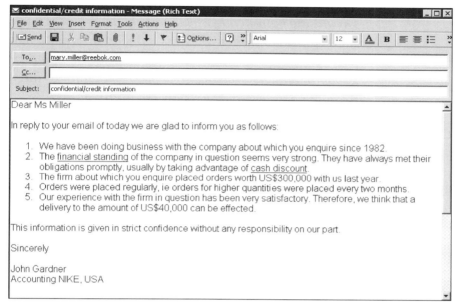

10.5 Text components

CI1   The above named have supplied your name as a trade reference. We would appreciate your answers to a few questions concerning the business conduct of the company.

We thank you for your assistance. Your reply will be treated with utmost confidentiality.

> *Sie wurden uns von der o.g. Firma als Handelsreferenz genannt. Wir würden uns freuen, wenn Sie uns ein paar Fragen bezüglich der Geschäftsgebaren des Unternehmens beantworten könnten.*
>
> *Vielen Dank für Ihre Mühe. Ihre Auskunft wird selbstverständlich streng vertraulich behandelt.*

CI2 As the firm in question is unknown to us, we would be grateful for information on their financial standing and their creditworthiness. What maximum credit may safely be granted in your opinion?

> *Da uns die betreffende Firma unbekannt ist, wären wir Ihnen dankbar, wenn Sie uns nähere Informationen über deren Finanzlage und deren Kreditwürdigkeit geben könnten. Welcher Höchstkredit könnte Ihrer Ansicht nach bedenkenlos gewährt werden?*

CI3 Please let us know whether in your opinion a credit limit of approx €50,000 would be reasonable. Your reply will be treated with utmost confidentiality. We can assure you of our future cooperation in any similar request from yourselves.

> *Bitte teilen Sie uns mit, ob Ihrer Ansicht nach ein Höchstkredit von ca. € 50.000,- vertretbar ist. Ihre Antwort wird streng vertraulich behandelt. Wir sind jederzeit gerne bereit, Ihnen in einer ähnlichen Angelegenheit Auskunft zu erteilen.*

CI4 We refer to your credit enquiry of 2 May 2005 and are glad to inform you that in our opinion, a delivery amounting to approx €50,000 can be safely effected.
This information is furnished in strict confidence without any responsibility on our part.

> *Wir beziehen uns auf Ihre Kreditanfrage vom 2. Mai 2005 und freuen uns, Ihnen mitzuteilen, dass eine Warensendung von ca. € 50.000,- unserer Ansicht nach bedenkenlos geliefert werden kann.*
>
> *Diese Auskunft ist streng vertraulich und wird ohne jegliche Haftung erteilt.*

CI5 We refer to your credit enquiry of 2 May 2005 and are glad to inform you that the firm in question is solvent for any credit required. We believe that you will not be taking any risk in granting them credit of up to approx €50,000.

This information is furnished in strict confidence without any responsibility on our part.

> *Wir beziehen uns auf Ihre Kreditanfrage vom 2. Mai 2005 und freuen uns, Ihnen mitzuteilen, dass die betreffende Firma für jeden Kredit solvent ist. Unserer Ansicht nach kann ein Kredit bis ca. € 50.000,- bedenkenlos gewährt werden.*
>
> *Diese Auskunft ist streng vertraulich und wird ohne jegliche Haftung erteilt.*

CI6   We refer to your credit enquiry of 2 May 2005 and are glad to inform you that the financial standing of the firm in question seems to be in order. Payments are effected as agreed upon, mostly by taking advantage of cash discount. Only in particular cases delays in payment have been noted. This information is furnished in strict confidence without any responsibility on our part.

> *Wir beziehen uns auf Ihre Kreditanfrage vom 2. Mai 2005 und freuen uns, Ihnen mitzuteilen, dass die finanziellen Verhältnisse der betreffenden Firma geordnet sind. Zahlungen erfolgen wie vereinbart, vorwiegend unter Skontoausnutzung. In Einzelfällen kam es zu Zielüberschreitungen. Diese Auskunft ist streng vertraulich und wird ohne jegliche Haftung erteilt.*

CI7   We refer to your credit enquiry of 2 May 2005. As the firm in question has been established only recently we are unable to express an opinion on their financial standing.

> *Wir beziehen uns auf Ihre Kreditanfrage vom 2. Mai 2005. Da die betreffende Firma erst kürzlich gegründet wurde, können wir keine Stellung zur Finanzlage dieser Firma nehmen.*

CI8   We refer to your credit enquiry of 2 May 2005 and regret to inform you that the financial standing of the firm in question is reported to be strained. Considerable delays in payment have been noted. The future development should be observed.

This information is furnished in strict confidence without any responsibility on our part.

Wir beziehen uns auf Ihre Kreditanfrage vom 2. Mai 2005 und bedauern, Ihnen mitteilen zu müssen, dass die Finanzlage der betreffenden Firma angespannt ist. Zahlungen erfolgen mit erheblichen Zielüberschreitungen. Die weitere Entwicklung sollte beobachtet werden. Diese Auskunft ist streng vertraulich und wird ohne jegliche Haftung erteilt.

CI9 We refer to your credit enquiry of 2 May 2005 and regret to inform you that we have been informed about a collection order against subject amounting to €75,000.

This information is furnished in strict confidence without any responsibility on our part.

Wir beziehen uns auf Ihre Kreditanfrage vom 2. Mai 2005 und bedauern, Ihnen mitteilen zu müssen, dass uns eine Mitteilung zu einem Inkassoverfahren über die betreffende Firma in Höhe von € 75.000,- vorliegt.

Diese Auskunft ist streng vertraulich und wird ohne jegliche Haftung erteilt.

CI10 We refer to your credit enquiry of 2 June and regret to inform you that we learnt from reliable sources that bankruptcy proceedings have been instituted at the district court on 1 May against subject. This information is furnished in strict confidence without any responsibility on our part.

Wir beziehen uns auf Ihre Kreditanfrage vom 2. Juni und bedauern, Ihnen mitteilen zu müssen, dass wir aus sicherer Quelle erfahren haben, dass am 1. Mai das Konkursverfahren beim Amtsgericht gegen die betreffende Firma eröffnet wurde. Diese Auskunft ist streng vertraulich und wird ohne jegliche Haftung erteilt.

10.6 Tasks

Please write emails using the following details and make use of the text components wherever you can:

10.6.1 Microsoft Corp, USA to Apple Company, USA

- Betreff/ Anrede
- Vertraulich/Kreditanfrage
- Saturn in Köln hat Ihnen als Handelsreferenz Apple Company Inc. genannt.
- Da bisher keine Geschäftsverbindung zu Saturn bestand, bitten Sie um Auskunft über deren Finanzlage und Zahlungsmoral.
- Fragen Sie an:
  a) Wie lange besteht die Geschäftsbeziehung zu Saturn und welcher Höchstkredit wurde bisher gewährt?
  b) Welche Umsätze wurden mit der betreffenden Firma in den letzten drei Jahren erzielt?
  c) Kann ein Kredit in Höhe von US$ 300.000,- sicher gewährt werden?
- Für jede weitere Auskunft, die Ihnen Apple Company Inc. geben kann, wären Sie dankbar.
- Sichern Sie vertrauliche Behandlung der Auskunft zu.
- Zu Gegendiensten sind Sie gerne bereit.
- Schlusssatz

10.6.2 Apple Company, USA to Microsoft Corp, USA

- Betreff/Anrede
- Vertraulich/Kreditauskunft
- Die betreffende Firma genießt einen guten Ruf und zählt zu den Branchenführern für innovative Elektroartikel mit mehr als 90 Märkten in Deutschland.
- Sie stehen seit mehr als 10 Jahren mit der betreffenden Firma in Geschäftsverbindung.

- Die finanziellen Verhältnisse sind geordnet. Während dieser 10 Jahre kam es nur in Einzelfällen zu Zielüberschreitungen, ansonsten ist die Firma ihren Verpflichtungen immer pünktlich nachgekommen, vorwiegend unter Skontoausnutzung.
- Die Umsätze der letzten drei Geschäftsjahre beliefen sich auf ca. ...
- Ihrer Meinung nach ist ein Kredit in Höhe von US$ 300.000,- vertretbar.
- Sie bitten um vertrauliche Behandlung der Auskunft.
- Sie erteilen die Auskunft ohne jegliche Haftung.
- Schlusssatz

10.6.3 Fill in the missing prepositions

1. As the firm ... question is unknown ... us, we would be grateful ... any information ... the company's past and present business conduct ... yourselves.
2. Your reply will be treated ... utmost confidentiality.
3. We think that you will not be running any risk ... granting them credit ... the extent of US$500,000.
4. A delivery ... the amount ... US$100,000 can be effected.
5. This information is furnished ... any responsibility ... our part.
6. We regret having to inform you that we are unable to express an opinion ... the financial standing ... the firm ... question.
7. As we have learnt ... reliable sources bankruptcy proceedings have been instituted ... the district court ... 15 May 2005.
8. Payments are effected as agreed ... , mostly ... taking advantage ... cash discount.
9. We have been informed ... a collection order ... the firm ... question.
10. We can assure you ... our future cooperation ... any similar request ... yourselves.

UNIT 11   CONFIRMING AN ORDER

11.1 Key facts

In foreign trade, if requested by the buyer, the seller confirms the buyer's order after receipt by sending an order confirmation or acknowledgement to the buyer repeating the essential points of his order. If payment by documentary letter of credit (L/C) is agreed, the seller sends a proforma-invoice to the buyer enabling him to present it to his bankers for opening of L/C.

11.1.1 Proforma-invoice

A proforma-invoice **does not demand payment**. It is primarily issued for customs purposes, eg
- For sending samples free of charge
- For sending replacements free of charge (guarantee or goodwill)
- For opening of L/C in the importing country
- For applying for an import licence in the importing country

Invoice forms are marked PROFORMA-INVOICE. If samples, replacement material or spare parts are sent abroad, the proforma-invoice also indicates:
- No commercial value
- Delivery free of charge
- For customs purposes only

11.2 Emails
11.2.1 Reebok, USA to Sportarena, Germany

Dear Mr Zoellner

Thank you for your order no 2234/03 of March 25, 2005 for running shoes. Please find attached our proforma-invoice.
Information on our General Terms and Conditions and Guaranty can be found at www.reebok.com

We have already started processing your order and we will do our best to have the goods ready for shipment by the end of this week.

Best regards

Tony Hancock
Sales Manager
Reebok International Ltd, USA

PROFORMA-INVOICE	dated March 26, 2005			Your order no 2234/03	
Quantity	Item		Size	Unit Price in US$	Amount in US$
20	1388742 *Reebok Premier Ultra DMX Running Shoe Men*		42	109.99	2,199.80
20	ditto		43	109.99	2,199.80
20	ditto		44	109.99	2,199.80
10	ditto		45	109.99	1,099.90
10	1388741 *Reebok Premier Ultra DMX Running Shoe Women*		37	109.99	1,099.90
20	ditto		38	109.99	2,199.80
20	ditto		39	109.99	2,199.80
20	ditto		40	109.99	2,199.80
10	ditto		41	109.99	1,099.90
20	1328542 *Reebok Premier Road Plus Running Shoe Men*		42	109.99	1,599.80
20	ditto		43	79.99	1,599.80
20	ditto		44	79.99	1,599.80
10	ditto		45	79.99	799.90
10	1328541 *Reebok Premier Road Plus Running Shoe Women*		37	79.99	799.90
20	ditto		38	79.99	1,599.80
20	ditto		39	79.99	1,599.80

Quantity	Item	Size	Unit Price in US$	Amount in US$
20	ditto	40	79.99	1,599.80
10	ditto	41	79.99	799.90
20	1427402 *Reebok circa Casual Shoe Men*	42	69.99	1,399.80
20	ditto	43	69.99	1,399.80
20	ditto	44	69.99	1,399.80
10	ditto	45	69.99	699.90
10	1427401 *Reebok circa Casual Shoe Women*	37	69.99	699.90
20	ditto	38	69.99	1,399.80
20	ditto	39	69.99	1,399.80
20	ditto	40	69.99	1,399.80
10	ditto	41	69.99	699.90
		total		US$38,995.50
		./. 20% special discount		US$7,799.10
		total amount FOB		**US$31,196.40**
		+ freight		**US$3,000.00**
		+ insurance		**US$200.00**
		total value CIF Hamburg		**US$34,396.40**

Shipping instructions: through Transamerican to Schenker, Boston by sea freight to the port of Hamburg

Terms of Delivery: CIF Hamburg

Terms of Payment: L/C to be opened in our favor at the Bank of America, Boston, USA, only

Bank details: Bank of America, Boston, USA
Account no 7 038 702
SWIFT BOFAUS3N

Delivery: after receipt of notification on opening of L/C

11.2.2 Twinings, UK to Broken English Berlin, Germany

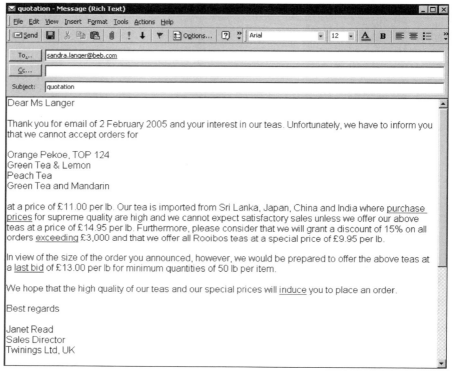

Dear Ms Langer

Thank you for email of 2 February 2005 and your interest in our teas. Unfortunately, we have to inform you that we cannot accept orders for

Orange Pekoe, TOP 124
Green Tea & Lemon
Peach Tea
Green Tea and Mandarin

at a price of £11.00 per lb. Our tea is imported from Sri Lanka, Japan, China and India where purchase prices for supreme quality are high and we cannot expect satisfactory sales unless we offer our above teas at a price of £14.95 per lb. Furthermore, please consider that we will grant a discount of 15% on all orders exceeding £3,000 and that we offer all Rooibos teas at a special price of £9.95 per lb.

In view of the size of the order you announced, however, we would be prepared to offer the above teas at a last bid of £13.00 per lb for minimum quantities of 50 lb per item.

We hope that the high quality of our teas and our special prices will induce you to place an order.

Best regards

Janet Read
Sales Director
Twinings Ltd, UK

11.3 Text components

CO1 Thank you for your order no 2234 dated 2 July 2005. Attached we are sending you the corresponding order confirmation as requested. We will notify you by email when the consignment is ready for collection.

> *Vielen Dank für Ihren Auftrag Nr. 2234 vom 2. Juli 2005. Als Dateianhang senden wir Ihnen wunschgemäß unsere Auftragbestätigung. Wir werden Sie per E-Mail informieren, sobald die Sendung abholbereit ist.*

CO2 Thank you for your order no 2234 of 2 July 2005. Attached please find our proforma-invoice enabling you to open L/C.
We have already started processing your order, and we will do our best to have the goods ready for shipment by the beginning of August.

> *Vielen Dank für Ihren Auftrag Nr. 2234 vom 2. Juli 2005. Als Dateianhang senden wir Ihnen unsere Proforma-Rechnung zur Akkreditiveröffnung.*
> *Wir haben bereits mit der Fertigung Ihres Auftrags begonnen und werden uns bemühen, die Waren bis Anfang August versandbereit zu haben.*

CO3 Thank you for your order no 2234 of 2 July 2005. Attached please find our proforma-invoice enabling you to apply for an import licence.
We will notify you by email when the consignment is ready for shipment.

> *Vielen Dank für Ihren Auftrag Nr. 2234 vom 2. Juli 2005. Als Dateianhang senden wir Ihnen unsere Proforma-Rechnung zur Beantragung der Importlizenz.*
> *Wir werden Sie per E-Mail informieren, sobald die Sendung versandbereit ist.*

CO4 We regret having to inform you that *hp 930a* printer is no longer available. However, we could substitute a similar product, our *hp 925c* printer, at the same price.

> *Wir bedauern, Ihnen mitteilen zu müssen, dass der Drucker hp 930a nicht mehr lieferbar ist. Wir können Ihnen jedoch ersatzweise ein ähnliches Produkt, unseren Drucker hp 925c, zum gleichen Preis anbieten.*

CO5 We regret to inform you that we are out of running shoes *Reebok Premier Road Plus*. Since this item will not be available until the beginning of August 2005, we could substitute a similar article, our running shoe *Reebok Premier Ultra DMX*, at the same price.

Wir bedauern, Ihnen mitteilen zu müssen, dass der Laufschuh Reebok Premier Road Plus ausverkauft ist. Da dieser Artikel erst Anfang August 2005 wieder vorrätig ist, bieten wir Ihnen ersatzweise einen ähnlichen Artikel, unseren Laufschuh Reebok Premier Ultra DMX, zum gleichen Preis an.

CO6 We regret to inform you that we cannot supply the teas at the prices indicated by you. Please note that the prices for tea mentioned in your order have been taken from last year's price list, which has recently been superseded by a new one.

Enclosed we are sending you our current price list along with our new catalogue. We kindly ask you to confirm your order at the current prices.

Wir bedauern, Ihnen mitteilen zu müssen, dass wir den Tee nicht zu den von Ihnen angegebenen Preisen liefern können. Die in Ihrem Auftrag genannten Preise basieren auf der Preisliste des letzten Jahres, die kürzlich durch eine neue ersetzt wurde.

Als Anlage senden wir Ihnen unsere aktuelle Preisliste zusammen mit unserem neuen Katalog. Bitte bestätigen Sie Ihren Auftrag zu den derzeit gültigen Preisen.

11.4 Tasks

Please confirm orders by email using the following details and make use of the text components wherever you can:

11.4.1 Microsoft Corp, USA to Saturn, Germany

- Betreff/Anrede
- Sie danken für die E-Mail vom … und das Interesse an *Microsoft Office Small Business Edition 2003 OEM-Version* und *Office Edition 2003 für Schüler, Studenten und Lehrkräfte* für die Sonderaktion vor der *CeBIT*.

- Eine Preisreduzierung von 15% ab 5.000 *Office Small Business Edition 2003* kann gewährt werden, wenn nach der *CeBIT* ein Folgeauftrag über mindestens 500 *Office Small Business Edition 2005 OEM-Version* in Aussicht gestellt wird. Einführungspreis: US$ 149,- pro Artikel.
- Lieferung: CIP Flughafen Köln/Bonn.
- Zahlung: CAD.
- Liefertermin: sofort nach Auftragserhalt.
- Sie bitten um Bestätigung.
- Schlusssatz

11.4.2 Durable, Germany to Office Supplies, Saudi Arabia

- Betreff/Anrede
- Sie danken für den Probeauftrag vom ... über Klemmhefter.
- Sie senden als Dateianhang die gewünschte Proforma-Rechnung.
- Sie bitten um schnellstmögliche L/C-Eröffnung.
- Schlusssatz
- Erstellen Sie als Dateianhang die Proforma-Rechnung.

11.4.3 Fill in the missing prepositions

1. We will notify you ... email as soon as your order no 3455 is ready ... shipment.
2. Just a quick note to inform you that your order no 3455 is ready ... collection.
3. We have already started processing your order, and we will do our best to have the goods ready ... shipment ... the beginning of August 2005.
4. Attached please find our proforma-invoice enabling you to apply ... an import licence.
5. We cannot execute your order no 3213 ... the prices stated ... you.
6. Unfortunately, we cannot deliver the running shoe *Reebok Premier Ultra Mens* or *Womens* directly ... stock.

7. We regret having to inform you that we are out … iced teas. New iced teas will not be available … the beginning of May 2005.

8. … *Green Tea and Lemon* we could substitute *Green Tea and Mandarin*, which has proved to be very popular in summer.

9. We have to inform you that the prices stipulated … your order no 3322 have been taken … last year's price list, which has recently been superseded … a new one.

10. We kindly ask you to confirm your order no 3322 … 2 June 2005… the current prices.

UNIT 12   ARRANGING A SHIPMENT

12.1 Key facts

When delivery is effected, the goods have to be accompanied by certain documents according to the <u>regulations</u> in the importer's country. Detailed information can be looked up in an <u>export reference book</u>. In Germany it is *K&M*[8].

As a rule, every <u>consignment</u> to be exported has to be accompanied by a <u>commercial invoice</u>. That is why commercial invoices and <u>proforma-invoices</u> are the most frequently issued documents in foreign trade.

12.2 Documents in foreign trade
12.2.1 Commercial invoice

The commercial invoice **demands payment** of a certain sum of money for goods delivered or services rendered.

The commercial invoice is the basis for <u>customs clearance</u> and statistical charge on imports. It serves as a supervision of foreign exchange. Additionally, it is the basis for issuing further shipping and insurance documents.

When issuing a commercial invoice both the regulations of the importing country and if necessary the conditions of the L/C have to be strictly <u>adhered to</u>. Details regarding the number of copies or the language of the commercial invoice required by the importing country are specified in *K&M*.

In international trade, all deliveries are <u>exempt from</u> sales tax, <u>subject to</u> proof of export, eg <u>consignment note</u>/<u>way bill</u>, <u>airway bill</u>, etc. Therefore, all invoices are issued net.

They should contain the following details:
- Name and address of exporter (usually indicated in the invoice form)
- <u>Bank details</u> of the exporter
- Full address of importer
- Invoice no and date
- Precise description of goods

[8] K&M = Konsulats- und Mustervorschriften;
    export reference book of the Chamber of Commerce in Hamburg

- Unit price, total price, additional costs for packing, transport and insurance
- Terms of delivery (Incoterms 2000)
- Terms of payment
- Mode of transport indicating airway bill no or B/L no
- Packing details
- Shipping marks

12.2.2 Packing list

If the goods are ready for shipment, the seller will take care of the export packaging and issue a packing list for each consignment indicating the following:

- Item no
- Precise description of goods
- Number of packages
- Type of package
- Contents of package
- Gross weight
- Net weight

Depending on the nature of the goods, types of packaging range from wooden cases, cardboard boxes, bags, bales, drums, barrels[2], and pallets to containers.

12.2.3 Certificate of Origin (C/O)

If required by the customs authorities of the importing country or if explicitly stated in the L/C, a Certificate of Origin has to be issued by the seller and signed by the seller's local Chamber of Commerce. The undersigned authority certifies that the goods described in the certificate originate in the country stipulated in the certificate.

The mark "Made in …" serves as consumer protection in the country of destination.

A Certificate of Origin contains the following details:

- Full address of exporter
- Full address of importer
- Country of origin

---

[9] A barrel is a round container for liquids that is wider in the middle than at the top and bottom.
In the oil industry, a barrel is a unit of measurement equivalent to 159 litres.

- Mode of transport
- Import licence no, L/C no, order no
- Number and type of packages
- Description of goods
- Quantities and weights
- Declaration if goods were manufactured in the company of the exporter or another company or if just a part of the goods was manufactured in the exporter's company. In the latter case, evidence has to be given where the remaining goods were manufactured.

12.2.4 Bill of Lading (B/L)

A document issued by a shipping company for transport of goods by sea. B/Ls are issued in a set of 3 originals signed by the master of the ship. On presentation of one of the originals, the master is instructed to release the goods. Afterwards, the remaining 2 originals become void.

Clean B/L: The B/L does **not** contain clauses or notations expressly declaring that the goods and/or the packaging are defective.

Unclean B/L: Clauses or notations such as the above appear in the B/L.

12.2.5 Airway Bill

A document issued by an airfreight company for transport by air. As rates for air transport are higher than those for sea transport, sensitive products such as computers, high quality goods such as electronic devices and expensive goods such as musical instruments are generally transported by air.

12.2.6 Consignment note or way bill

A document issued by the exporter and acknowledged by the first carrier when the goods are handed over to him for transport by road.

12.3 Marks
12.3.1 Shipping marks

Additionally, shipping marks are labelled on each packing unit to ensure that the goods reach the agreed destination. Unless otherwise advised by the buyer, the seller will indicate the following <u>irremovable</u> and <u>indelible</u> standard marks:

Seller's abbreviation/order no/country of destination

	REEBOK/13201/GERMANY
Number of packages	**No 1-25**
<u>Country of Origin</u>	**MADE IN USA**

12.3.2 Caution marks

If requested by the importer, caution marks will be added to each packing unit. The most frequently used ones are as follows:

fragile, keep dry, keep in cool place, store away from heat, inflammable, poison, radioactive, this side up, handle with care, do not bend.

12.4 Emails

12.4.1 Reebok, USA to Sportarena, Germany

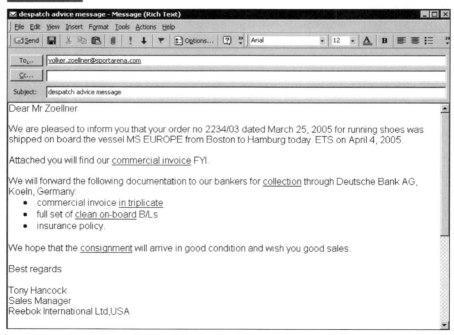

12.4.2 Twinings, UK to Broken English Berlin, Germany

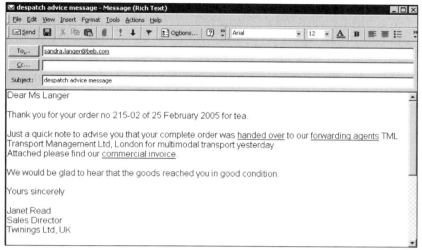

```
despatch advice message - Message (Rich Text)                    _ □ ×
File  Edit  View  Insert  Format  Tools  Actions  Help
Send  ⊟  ⅛ ⓑ ⓑ  ⓤ  !  ↓  ⓨ  Options...  ?  »  Arial        ▼  12  ▼  A  B  ≡ ≡ ⋮≡  »

To...    sandra.langer@beb.com
Cc...
Subject: despatch advice message

Dear Ms Langer

Thank you for your order no 215-02 of 25 February 2005 for tea.

Just a quick note to advise you that your complete order was handed over to our forwarding agents TML
Transport Management Ltd, London for multimodal transport yesterday.
Attached please find our commercial invoice.

We would be glad to hear that the goods reached you in good condition.

Yours sincerely

Janet Read
Sales Director
Twinings Ltd, UK
```

12.5 Text components

AS1   Referring to your above order, please note that we have applied for L/C at the Bank of America, New York.
Please let us know when the goods are expected to be shipped.

> *Wir beziehen uns auf Ihren o.g. Auftrag und möchten Ihnen mitteilen, dass das L/C bei der Bank of America in New York beantragt wurde.*
> *Bitte lassen Sie uns wissen, wann die Ware voraussichtlich verschifft wird.*

AS2   Just a quick note to inform you that we received a copy of the L/C from our bankers. We have already started packing the goods, and they are expected to be shipped in about a fortnight. Details will follow.

> *Wir möchten Sie kurz informieren, dass wir inzwischen von unserer Bank eine L/C-Kopie erhalten haben. Die Ware wird bereits gepackt. Verschiffung wird in ca. 14 Tagen geplant. Details folgen.*

AS3   We are pleased to inform you that the goods were shipped today in conformity with the L/C on board the vessel MS EUROPE ex Hamburg, ETA in New York on 24 September 2005.

Attached please find a copy of our commercial invoice FYI.

We will forward the documentation (B/L, commercial invoice, packing list, and C/O) to our bankers for collection through the Bank of America, New York.

We hope that the goods will reach you in good condition and wish you good sales.

> *Wir freuen uns, Ihnen mitzuteilen, dass die Waren heute L/C-konform an Bord der MS EUROPE ab Hamburg verschifft wurden. Voraussichtliche Ankunft in New York am 24. September 2005.*
>
> *Anbei senden wir Ihnen eine Kopie unserer Rechnung zur Ihrer Information.*
>
> *Die Dokumente (B/L, Exportrechnung, Packliste und C/O), werden über unsere Bank an die Bank of America in New York zum Zahlungseinzug eingereicht.*
>
> *Wir hoffen, dass die Waren in einwandfreiem Zustand bei Ihnen ankommen und wünschen Ihnen viel Erfolg beim Verkauf.*

AS4   We are pleased to inform you that your above order has today been handed over to our forwarding agents SCHENKER, Düsseldorf, for transport by air from Düsseldorf to Mexico City, ETA on 24 September 2005.

The shipping papers will be sent to you by FedEx.

We hope that the goods will reach you in good condition.

> *Wir freuen uns, Ihnen mitzuteilen, dass Ihr o.g. Auftrag heute unserem Spediteur, SCHENKER, Düsseldorf, zum Transport per Luftfracht von Düsseldorf nach Mexico City am 24. September übergeben wurde. Voraussichtliche Ankunft am 24. September 2005.*
>
> *Die Versandpapiere werden Ihnen per FedEx zugesandt.*
>
> *Wir hoffen, dass die Waren in einwandfreiem Zustand bei Ihnen ankommen.*

AS5 We are pleased to inform you that your above order is ready for collection. Please let us have your instructions asap.

>*Wir freuen uns, Ihnen mitzuteilen, dass Ihr obiger Auftrag abholbereit ist. Bitte teilen Sie uns baldmöglichst Ihre Anweisungen mit.*

AS6 We hereby certify that the goods are of pure German origin and that the goods are manufactured by Durable GmbH & CO KG, Germany.

>*Hiermit bestätigen wir, dass die Waren reinen deutschen Ursprungs sind und dass diese von Durable GmbH & CO. KG, Deutschland, hergestellt wurden.*

12.6 Tasks

Please send <u>despatch advice messages</u> by email using the following details and make use of the text components wherever you can:

12.6.1 Microsoft Corp, USA to Saturn, Germany

- Betreff/Anrede
- Sie danken für Auftrag Nr. 22445 vom ... über 5.000 *Office Small Business Edition 2003 OEM-Version* und 5.000 *Office Edition für Schüler, Studenten und Lehrkräfte.*
- Sie teilen mit, dass die Ware bereits gepackt wird.
- Der Versand per Luftfracht wird in ca. 5 Tagen geplant; Details folgen.
- Schlusssatz

12.6.2 Durable, Germany to Office Supplies, Saudi Arabia

- Betreff/Anrede
- Sie nehmen Bezug auf den Probeauftrag vom ... über Klemmhefter.
- Die Ware ist heute L/C-konform mit MS ROYAL STAR ab Hamburg verschifft worden.
- Voraussichtliche Ankunft in Djidda: 15. August 2005.
- Anbei senden Sie Kopien der Packliste und der Rechnung zur Info.

- Die Original-Versandpapiere werden über Ihre Bank an die Standard Chartered Bank in Djidda zum Zahlungseinzug eingereicht.
- Sie wünschen einen guten Empfang der Ware und viel Erfolg beim Verkauf.
- Schlusssatz

12.6.3 Fill in the missing prepositions

1. We need a proforma-invoice ... presentation ... the import control authorities when applying ... an import licence.
2. Please let us know if dimensions, gross and net weights are to be labelled ... the packing units.
3. Your order has been handed ... ... our forwarding agents, ATEGE Group Logistics, Cologne, ... transport ... road.
4. Will you arrange ... the collection of the shipment ... our Cologne works?
5. All items were carefully checked prior ... shipment and we hope they will reach you ... good condition.
6. The shipping papers will be sent to you ... courier service.
7. We are pleased to advise you that your order no 224 was shipped ... board the vessel MS COLUMBUS ... New York ... Hamburg. ETA ... 14 May 2005.
8. Attached please find a copy of our commercial invoice ... your information.
9. The documentation has been forwarded ... our bankers ... collection ... the Bank of America.
10. We hereby certify that the goods are ... pure national origin ... the exporting country and that the goods are manufactured ... Messrs Durable, Germany.

UNIT 13   EFFECTING PAYMENT

13.1 Key facts

Contrary to business in domestic trade, where payment is effected by sending an <u>invoice</u>, the buyer in foreign trade often needs a variety of documents to undertake importing the goods. Therefore, it is of great importance to agree on the documents required for the payment of the goods at the offer phase.

> There is a general difference in meaning between bill and invoice.
> **Bill:** a general term for services rendered, work done and goods sent.
> **Invoice:** just relates to goods sent in commerce.

13.2 Factoring

Factoring is used to describe a range of financial products where finance is provided against invoices.

Typically as an invoice is raised a copy will be sent to a factoring company, the factor, who will then <u>fund up</u> to 90% against the invoice in advance of the customer paying, less a fee of approx 3% of the invoice amount. The remainder will become payable on a <u>maturity date</u> or when the customer pays. As the invoice is assigned to the factoring company, payment by the customer will be direct to the factoring company.

Factoring is suitable for companies who offer goods on credit terms. By providing up to 90% finance against invoices, factoring can bridge the gap between the <u>raising of an invoice</u> and getting that invoice paid.

For more information on factoring please visit <u>www.globalfinanceonline.com</u>.

13.3 Emails

13.3.1 Sportarena, Germany to Reebok, USA

order no 4582 for Soccer Mens - Message (Rich Text)

File Edit View Insert Format Tools Actions Help

Send | Options... | Arial | 12 | A B

To.. | tony.hancock@reebok.com

Cc...

Subject: order no 4582 for Soccer Mens

Dear Mr Hancock

Yesterday we received our above order for 200 soccer shoes *Reebok Baleni III* and 200 soccer shoes *Reebok Royal Match* and thank you for the prompt delivery.

Payment of your invoice no 13110 of May 25, 2005 will be effected by SWIFT.

Best regards

Volker Zöllner
Sportarena, Germany

13.3.2 Twinings, UK to Broken English Berlin, Germany

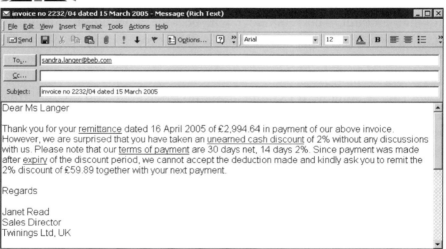

invoice no 2232/04 dated 15 March 2005 - Message (Rich Text)

File Edit View Insert Format Tools Actions Help

Send | Options... | Arial | 12 | A B

To.. | sandra.langer@beb.com

Cc...

Subject: invoice no 2232/04 dated 15 March 2005

Dear Ms Langer

Thank you for your remittance dated 16 April 2005 of £2,994.64 in payment of our above invoice. However, we are surprised that you have taken an unearned cash discount of 2% without any discussions with us. Please note that our terms of payment are 30 days net, 14 days 2%. Since payment was made after expiry of the discount period, we cannot accept the deduction made and kindly ask you to remit the 2% discount of £59.89 together with your next payment.

Regards

Janet Read
Sales Director
Twinings Ltd, UK

13.4 Text components

P1   Just a quick note to inform you that we received the goods of the above order in good condition.

We have instructed our bankers today to remit the amount of your invoice no 14567 of May 3, 2005 to your account with the Bank of America, New York. **(AE)**

> *Wir möchten Sie nur kurz darüber informieren, dass die Waren des o.g. Auftrages in einwandfreiem Zustand bei uns eingegangen sind.*
>
> *Wir haben heute unsere Bank angewiesen, den Betrag Ihrer Rechnung Nr. 14567 vom 3. Mai 2005 auf Ihr Konto bei der Bank of America in New York zu überweisen.*

P2   Thank you for the prompt delivery of our above order. The goods arrived in good condition.

In the meantime, we have checked your invoice and have settled payment by SWIFT.

> *Danke für die schnelle Lieferung unseres o.g. Auftrags. Die Waren sind in einwandfreiem Zustand bei uns eingetroffen.*
>
> *In der Zwischenzeit haben wir Ihre Rechnung geprüft und Zahlung per SWIFT veranlasst.*

P3   Please note that there is a discrepancy between the number of items delivered and the number of items charged in your invoice no 234 of 10 April 2005. We ordered and received 1,000 plastic folders of item no 2202 but were charged 1,000 boxes of item no 2202. Please check your records and let us have your comments asap.

> *Die Anzahl der gelieferten Waren stimmt nicht mit der Anzahl der berechneten Waren in Ihrer Rechnung Nr. 234 vom 10. April 2005 überein. Wir bestellten und erhielten 1.000 Stück Schnellhefter Nr. 2202. Uns wurden aber 1.000 Kartons Artikel Nr. 2202 berechnet. Bitte prüfen Sie Ihre Unterlagen und benachrichtigen Sie uns so schnell wie möglich.*

P4   When checking your remittance covering the above invoice we noted that there is a deviation in the exchange rate for US$ of 1.05 calculated by you and the official exchange rate of June 21, 2005 of 1.20. Please remit the difference to our account.

> *Bei Prüfung Ihrer Überweisung in Begleichung unserer o.g. Rechnung stellten wir fest, dass der von Ihnen angewandte Umrechnungskurs für US$ von 1,05 nicht mit dem offiziellen Kurs vom 21. Juni 2005 von 1,20 übereinstimmt. Bitte überweisen Sie den Differenzbetrag auf unser Konto.*

P5   We regret to inform you that you have taken an unearned cash discount of 2% on our above invoice. Since payment was made after expiry of the agreed cash discount period of 14 days, we cannot accept your deduction. Please send us a crossed cheque covering the difference.

> *Leider müssen wir Ihnen mitteilen, dass Sie einen unberechtigten Skontoabzug von 2% auf obige Rechnung vorgenommen haben. Da die Zahlung nach Ablauf der vereinbarten Barzahlungsfrist von 14 Tagen erfolgte, können wir den Abzug nicht mehr berücksichtigen. Bitte senden Sie uns einen Verrechnungsscheck über den Differenzbetrag.*

P6   We have assigned the invoice to our factoring company as specified in our General Terms and Conditions. Please effect payment directly to Dunhall Ltd, London, UK.

> *Wie bereits in unseren Allgemeinen Geschäftsbedingungen angegeben, haben wir die Rechnung an unsere Factoring Gesellschaft abgetreten. Wir bitten Sie, die Zahlung direkt an Dunhall Ltd, London, UK vorzunehmen.*

13.5 Tasks

Please write emails using the following details and make use of the text components wherever you can:

13.5.1 Saturn, Germany to Microsoft Corp, USA

- Betreff/ Anrede
- Sie danken für die schnelle Lieferung des Folgeauftrags Nr. 2445 vom ... über 1.000 Stück Software *Windows XP.*
- Die Sendung ist heute in einwandfreiem Zustand eingegangen.
- Bei Prüfung der Rechnung stellte sich heraus, dass Ihnen zu viel berechnet wurde. Anstatt 1.000 sind 1.500 Stück berechnet worden. Laut Wareneingang sind aber tatsächlich nur 1.000 Stück Software *Windows XP* geliefert worden.
- Sie bitten um Prüfung der Unterlagen und um Zusendung einer neuen Rechnung.
- Schlusssatz

13.5.2 Office Supplies, Saudi Arabia to Durable, Germany

- Betreff/Anrede
- Sie danken für die zufriedenstellende erste Geschäftsab-wicklung.
- Die Sendung ist wohlbehalten in Djidda eingetroffen.
- Sie würden gerne Folgeaufträge erteilen und erkundigen sich, ob auch Geschäfte zu anderen Zahlungsbedingungen möglich sind, z.B. Kasse gegen Dokumente.
- Bei der Standard Chartered Bank in Djidda, Saudi Arabien, kann eine Bankreferenz eingeholt werden.
- Sie bitten um Prüfung der Angelegenheit und um Stellungnahme.
- Schlusssatz

13.5.3 Fill in the missing prepositions

1. The goods were examined and turned out ... our complete satisfaction.
2. We regret to inform you that you have taken an unearned cash discount ... 2% ... our above invoice.
3. Since payment was made ... expiry .... the agreed cash discount period ... 14 days, we cannot accept your deduction.
4. ... payment ... the unearned cash discount taken we enclose a crossed cheque ... €60.10.
5. We have instructed our bankers to remit the amount ... US$32,000 ... your account ... the Bank of America, New York.
6. There is a discrepancy ... the number of items delivered and invoiced.
7. We have received your invoice ... €4,595.
8. There is a deviation ... the exchange rate ... US$ ... 1.05 calculated ... you and the official exchange rate ... June 21, 2005 ... 1.20.
9. The goods covered ... your invoice of 1 March 2005 arrived ... board the vessel MS EUROPE ... Hamburg yesterday.
10. Since we have assigned the invoice ... our factoring company, please effect payment directly ... Dunhall Ltd, London, UK.

UNIT 14   SENDING A DELIVERY REMINDER

14.1 Key facts

There are many reasons why delivery is not effected within the period agreed upon. The most frequent ones are mentioned below.

Before goods are <u>handed over</u> to the first carrier:
* <u>Acts of God</u>, eg war, flood, fire, strike or other circumstances beyond the seller's control
* Problems in manufacture, eg <u>equipment failure</u>, <u>poor quality output</u> necessitating reproduction
* Delayed supply of <u>raw material</u>

After goods are <u>handed over</u> to the first carrier:
* Breakdown or accidents of HGVs
* Missing flights or <u>vessels</u>
* Delayed departures due to bad weather or breakdown of machinery
* Loss of cargos

In any case, the buyer will remind the seller of the outstanding delivery and fix a new deadline. When missing this deadline, reminders will follow and after <u>expiry</u> of a second deadline, the seller must assume the cancellation of the order or the claim for damages.

There is a general difference in meaning between Act of God and <u>Force Majeure</u>:

Act of God is an old term for an extraordinary interruption of the usual course of events by a natural cause (as a flood or an earthquake) that could not be reasonably have been foreseen or prevented. **Force Majeure** is no longer limited to *Acts of God*. Typically, *Force Majeure* clauses cover natural disasters, war, <u>riot</u> or other major <u>political upheaval</u>, or the <u>failure</u> of third parties – such as suppliers and subcontractors – to perform their obligations to the contracting party. It is important to remember that *Force Majeure* clauses are intended to excuse a party only if failure to perform could not be avoided by the exercise of due care by that party!

For more information on *Force Majeure* clauses, see <u>www.library.yale.com</u>.

14.2 Emails

14.2.1 Sportarena, Germany to Reebok, USA

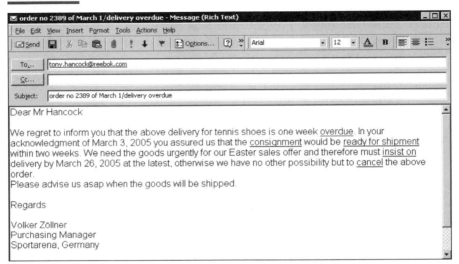

order no 2389 of March 1/delivery overdue - Message (Rich Text)

File Edit View Insert Format Tools Actions Help

Send | Options... | Arial | 12 | A B

To... | tony.hancock@reebok.com

Cc... |

Subject: | order no 2389 of March 1/delivery overdue

Dear Mr Hancock

We regret to inform you that the above delivery for tennis shoes is one week overdue. In your acknowledgment of March 3, 2005 you assured us that the consignment would be ready for shipment within two weeks. We need the goods urgently for our Easter sales offer and therefore must insist on delivery by March 26, 2005 at the latest, otherwise we have no other possibility but to cancel the above order.
Please advise us asap when the goods will be shipped.

Regards

Volker Zöllner
Purchasing Manager
Sportarena, Germany

14.2.2 Twinings, UK to Broken English Berlin, Germany

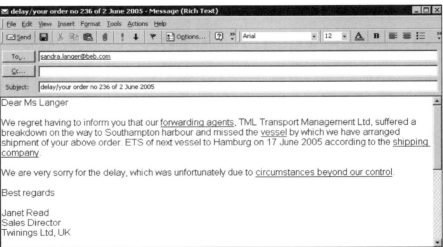

delay/your order no 236 of 2 June 2005 - Message (Rich Text)

File Edit View Insert Format Tools Actions Help

Send | Options... | Arial | 12 | A B

To... | sandra.langer@beb.com

Cc... |

Subject: | delay/your order no 236 of 2 June 2005

Dear Ms Langer

We regret having to inform you that our forwarding agents, TML Transport Management Ltd, suffered a breakdown on the way to Southampton harbour and missed the vessel by which we have arranged shipment of your above order. ETS of next vessel to Hamburg on 17 June 2005 according to the shipping company.

We are very sorry for the delay, which was unfortunately due to circumstances beyond our control.

Best regards

Janet Read
Sales Director
Twinings Ltd, UK

14.3 Text components

DR1   We regret to inform you that our above order is one week overdue. Please look into the matter and advise us when the goods will be shipped.

> *Wir bedauern, Ihnen mitteilen zu müssen, dass unser o.g. Auftrag eine Woche überfällig ist. Bitte prüfen Sie die Angelegenheit und teilen Sie uns mit, wann die Ware versandt wird.*

DR2   We explicitly stated in our order that the goods must reach us by the end of November at the latest, since we urgently need them for the Christmas season. Therefore, your delay in delivery places us in a difficult position.

> *Wir haben in unserer Bestellung ausdrücklich darauf hingewiesen, dass wir die Ware spätestens bis Ende November benötigen, da wir sie dringend für die Weihnachtssaison benötigen. Ihr Lieferverzug bringt uns daher in eine schwierige Lage.*

DR3   We are sorry for the delay of your above order. Unfortunately, machine failure has delayed our production. We will do our best, however, to have the goods ready for shipment by the beginning of next week.

You can be assured that we will take appropriate measures to avoid such delays in future.

> *Wir bedauern die Verzögerung Ihres o.g. Auftrags. Leider hat ein Maschinenausfall die Produktion aufgehalten. Wir werden jedoch unser Bestes tun, um die Ware Anfang nächster Woche versandbereit zu haben.*
>
> *Wir versichern Ihnen, dass wir die nötigen Maßnahmen ergreifen werden, um solche Verspätungen in Zukunft zu vermeiden.*

DR4   We regret to inform you that the departure of MS TRANSAMERICAN on which we have booked shipment of your above order could not sail because of stormy weather. ETS on 27 January 2005, according to the shipping company.

We regret the delay over which, however, we have no influence.

Wir bedauern Ihnen mitteilen zu müssen, dass die MS TRANSAMERICAN, mit der Ihre Ware verschifft werden sollte, aufgrund von Sturm nicht auslaufen konnte. Der Frachter soll laut der Reederei nun am 27. Januar 2005 auslaufen. Wir bedauern die Verzögerung, auf die wir aber keinen Einfluss haben.

DR5   Our above order is 8 weeks overdue now. We set two further deadlines for delivery. As you missed both deadlines, we are forced to cancel the above order. Please note that we must hold you liable for all losses incurred.

Unser obiger Auftrag ist nun 8 Wochen überfällig. Wir haben Ihnen zwei weitere Liefertermine gesetzt. Da Sie beide Liefertermine überschritten haben, sehen wir uns gezwungen, den Auftrag zu stornieren. Wir müssen Sie darauf aufmerksam machen, dass wir Sie für alle uns entstehenden Verluste haftbar machen.

DR6   We cannot accept your repeated delays in delivery any longer. If you cannot give us your definite promise that our above order will be shipped by the end of this week, we are compelled to cancel this and all outstanding orders.

Wir können Ihren ständigen Lieferverzug nicht länger akzeptieren. Wenn Sie uns nicht definitiv zusagen können, dass unser o.g. Auftrag bis Ende dieser Woche versandt wird, sehen wir uns gezwungen, diesen und alle noch ausstehenden Aufträge zu stornieren.

DR7 We regret to inform you that our forwarding agents suffered a breakdown in transit and missed the vessel by which we have arranged carriage of your above order. ETS of the next vessel will be on 2 May 2005.

We are very sorry for the delay, which was due to circumstances beyond our control.

Wir bedauern, Ihnen mitteilen zu müssen, dass unser Spediteur auf dem Transportweg eine LKW-Panne erlitt und den Frachter, mit dem Ihr obiger Auftrag verschifft werden sollte, verpasst hat. Voraussichtlicher Verschiffungstermin des nächsten Frachters: 2. Mai 2005.

Wir bedauern die Verspätung sehr, die auf Umstände zurückzuführen ist, auf die wir keinen Einfluss hatten.

14.4 Tasks

Please send <u>delivery reminders</u> by email using the following details and make use of the text components wherever you can:

14.4.1 Saturn, Germany to Microsoft Corp, USA

- Anrede/ Betreff
- Sie sind beunruhigt, weil Ihr Auftrag Nr. 2455 vom ... über 1.000 Stück Software *Windows XP* seit einer Woche überfällig ist, obwohl Lieferung ab Lager zugesagt wurde.
- Sie hatten in Ihrer Bestellung ausdrücklich darauf hingewiesen, dass die Ware spätestens bis zum 2. Februar 2005 eingehen muss, um diese für die von Ihnen geplante Verkaufsaktion vor der *CeBIT* anbieten zu können.
- Sie setzen eine letzte Lieferfrist bis zum 9. Februar 2005. Sollte der Auftrag bis dahin nicht ausgeliefert worden sein, sehen Sie sich gezwungen, diesen Auftrag zu stornieren.
- Sie bitten um Prüfung der Angelegenheit und um umgehende Nachricht, warum die Ware verspätet ist.
- Schlusssatz

14.4.2 Durable, Germany to Office Supplies, Saudi Arabia

- Betreff/Anrede
- Sie bedauern mitteilen zu müssen, dass der Auftrag Nr. 2221 vom ... über 500.000 Klarsichthüllen, Artikel Nr. 2339, nicht termingerecht versandt werden kann.
- Leider stellte sich nach der Produktion der Klarsichthüllen heraus, dass das Material fehlerhaft war.
- Sie haben vom Rohstofflieferanten bereits neues Material erhalten und müssen die Ware jetzt neu auflegen, um qualitativ hochwertige Erzeugnisse liefern zu können.
- Die Auslieferung wird sich dadurch um ca. 4 Wochen verzögern.
- Da die Importlizenz am 10. Juni 2005 abläuft, bitten Sie um Verlängerung.

- Sie entschuldigen sich für die entstandenen Unannehmlichkeiten und werden den o.g. Auftrag mit höchster Priorität
behandeln.
- Schlusssatz

14.4.3 Fill in the missing prepositions

1. We regret ... inform you that our order no 2245 ... 27 January
2005 is more than a week overdue.
2. Please look ... the matter and advise us when the goods will
be shipped.
3. We explicitly stated ... our order that the goods must reach us
... the end of October 2005 ... the latest.
4. Your delay ... delivery places us ... a difficult position.
5. We are very sorry ... the delay ... delivery.
6. MS PONT DAMIETTA ... which we have booked shipment
... your above order could not sail according ... schedule
because ... bad weather.
7. ETS ... Felixstowe ... 1 March 2005.
8. We regret the delay ... which, however, we have no
influence.
9. We are very sorry ... the delay, which was unfortunately due
... circumstances ... our control.
10. You can be assured that we will take appropriate measures to
avoid such delays ... future.

UNIT 15   MAKING COMPLAINTS

15.1 Key facts

On delivery of the <u>consignment</u>, the buyer's <u>goods receiving department</u> will examine the goods carefully regarding the quality and the quantity of the goods. If the results of the <u>goods inward test</u> are not satisfactory, the buyer will complain. The buyer's most frequent causes for <u>complaints</u> are as follows:

- <u>Poor quality</u> (minor quality, faulty goods, goods do not <u>correspond to</u> <u>samples</u> or <u>patterns</u>, material defect, etc)
- <u>Shortfalls</u> (<u>shortage in weight</u> or number of items)
- Damage <u>in transit</u>
- Loss in transit

15.2 Emails
15.2.1 Sportarena, Germany to Reebok, USA

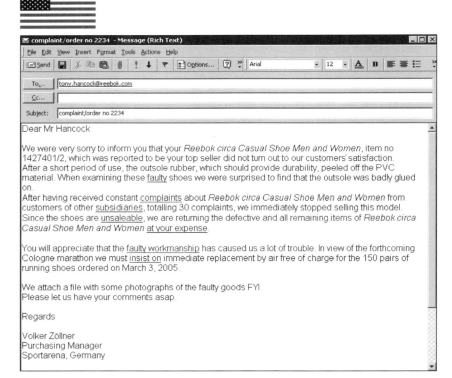

15.2.2 Broken English Berlin, Germany to Twinings, UK

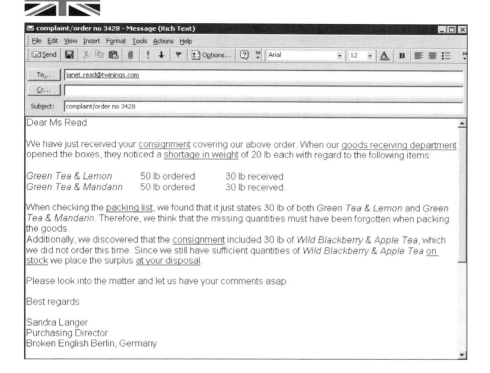

15.3 Text components

MC1 We have just examined your last consignment and noted that we actually received 1,800 instead of the 2,000 *hp 945c* printers that we ordered on June 25, 2005. Please look into the matter and let us have your comments regarding the missing 200 printers asap. **(AE)**

> *Wir haben gerade Ihre letzte Sendung geprüft und festgestellt, dass tatsächlich nur 1.800 der 2.000 am 25. Juni 2005 bestellten Drucker hp 945c geliefert wurden. Bitte prüfen Sie die Angelegenheit schnellstmöglich und nehmen Sie zu den fehlenden 200 Druckern Stellung.*

MC2 We have just received your last consignment of printers. After testing the *hp 945c* printers we noticed that the colour printings did not meet our standards. However, we are willing to keep the printers if you reduce the price by 15%.

> *Wir haben gerade Ihre letzte Sendung Drucker erhalten. Nachdem wir die Drucker hp 945c getestet haben, stellten wir fest, dass die Farbdrucke nicht unserem Standard entsprechen. Wir sind jedoch bereit, die Drucker zu behalten, wenn Sie den Preis um 15% reduzieren.*

MC3 We are sorry to inform you that our above order for *hp 945c* printers did not reach us in good condition. Part of the printers was damaged in transit. When opening the boxes we noted that the top covers of the printers were broken.
We are returning the damaged printers and ask you to have them repaired asap.

> *Wir müssen Ihnen leider mitteilen, dass unser o.g. Auftrag über die Drucker hp 945c nicht in einwandfreiem Zustand bei uns angekommen ist. Ein Teil der Drucker wurde auf dem Transportweg beschädigt. Beim Öffnen der Kartons stellten wir fest, dass die Abdeckungen der Drucker zerbrochen waren.*
>
> *Wir senden Ihnen die beschädigten Drucker zurück und bitten Sie, diese schnellstmöglich zu reparieren.*

MC4 We are sorry to inform you that our above order for *hp 945c* printers did not reach us in good condition. When opening the boxes we noted that the top covers of the printers were broken. We suppose that the damage was caused by inappropriate packaging. Attached please find a file including a photograph of the damage.
We are placing the damaged printers at your disposal and await your instructions.
Any further business will depend on how you settle this matter.

Wir müssen Ihnen leider mitteilen, dass unser o.g. Auftrag über Drucker hp 945c nicht in einwandfreiem Zustand bei uns angekommen ist. Beim Öffnen der Kartons stellten wir fest, dass die Abdeckungen der Drucker zerbrochen waren. Wir vermuten, dass der Schaden auf unzureichende Verpackung zurückzuführen ist. Als Dateianhang erhalten Sie ein Foto des Schadens. Wir stellen Ihnen die defekten Drucker zur Verfügung und erwarten Ihre Anweisungen.
Weitere Geschäfte werden davon abhängen, wie Sie diese Angelegenheit regeln.

MC5 We are sorry to inform you that our above order for *hp 945c* printers did not reach us in good condition. When opening the boxes we noted that the top covers of the printers were broken. Since the damaged *hp 945c* printers are unsaleable, we are returning them at your expense and kindly ask you to send us a credit note.

Wir müssen Ihnen leider mitteilen, dass unser o.g. Auftrag über Drucker hp 945c nicht in einwandfreiem Zustand bei uns angekommen ist. Beim Öffnen der Kartons stellten wir fest, dass die Abdeckungen der Drucker zerbrochen waren. Da die beschädigten Drucker hp 945c unverkäuflich sind, senden wir Ihnen diese auf Ihre Kosten zurück und bitten um Zusendung einer Gutschrift.

MC6 We are sorry to inform you that our above order for *hp 945c* printers did not reach us in good condition. When opening the boxes we noted that the top covers of 60 printers were broken. We are sending you samples of the damaged printers as evidence and ask you to send us replacements asap.

Wir müssen Ihnen leider mitteilen, dass unser o.g. Auftrag über Drucker hp 945c nicht in einwandfreiem Zustand bei uns angekommen ist. Beim Öffnen der Kartons stellten wir fest, dass die Abdeckungen von

*60 Druckern zerbrochen waren. Wir senden Ihnen
Muster der defekten Drucker als Beweis zu und bitten
um schnellstmöglichen Ersatz.*

15.4 Tasks

Please make <u>complaints</u> by email using the following details and
make use of the text components wherever you can:

15.4.1 Saturn, Germany to Microsoft Corp, USA

- Betreff/Anrede
- Sie haben heute die letzte Sendung Software *Windows XP*
  erhalten, auf die Sie schon lange gewartet haben.
- Beim Wareneingang wurde aber festgestellt, dass tatsächlich
  nur 4 der 5 auf der Packliste und im Luftfrachtbrief aufgeführten
  Paletten bei Ihnen angekommen sind.
- Eine Palette mit 200 Stück Software *Windows XP* fehlte.
- Sie nehmen daher an, dass die Ware auf dem Transportweg
  verloren gegangen ist.
- Sie bitten um Prüfung der Angelegenheit und um
  schnellstmögliche Stellungnahme.
- Schlusssatz

15.4.2 Office Supplies, Saudi Arabia to Durable, Germany

- Betreff/Anrede
- Sie haben gerade die Sendung über 500.000 Klarsichthüllen
  erhalten und sind leider mit der Ware nicht zufrieden.
- Beim Öffnen der Kartons, stellten Sie fest, dass die Ware in der
  Verpackung zerknittert war und die Ecken der Klarsichthüllen
  umgebogen waren.
- Als Beweis schicken Sie per Luftpost einige beschädigte
  Klarsichthüllen.
- Da Sie die mangelhafte Ware nicht verkaufen können,
  stellen Sie diese Durable zur Verfügung und erwarten deren
  Anweisungen.

- Sie bitten schnellstmöglich um eine kostenlose Ersatzlieferung, da Ihr Lagerbestand an Klarsichthüllen fast erschöpft ist.
- Sie bitten um Prüfung der Angelegenheit und um umgehende Stellungnahme.
- Schlusssatz

15.4.3 Fill in the missing prepositions

1. We regret to inform you that the flat screens did not turn out … our satisfaction.
2. Part of the printers was also damaged … transit.
3. We are sending you samples of the damaged printers … evidence and ask you to send us replacements asap.
4. We have no use … the faulty flat screens and place them … your disposal.
5. Attached please find a file showing a photograph … the damaged printers.
6. We cannot keep the flat screens, unless you reduce the price … 15%.
7. Please send us replacements … the printers asap.
8. We suppose that the damage was caused … inappropriate packaging.
9. We are returning the printers … your expense.
10. Please note that any further business will depend … how you settle this matter.

UNIT 16   DEALING WITH COMPLAINTS

16.1 Key facts

The seller should quickly examine the <u>complaint</u> he receives. If it is justified he will make up for the damage or loss, replace goods or send <u>substitutes</u>. If the buyer's complaint is unjustified, the seller may refuse the complaint. However, in case of an important key customer, he might be willing to grant the claim because of <u>goodwill</u>. In fact, it is much easier to keep a customer than to acquire a new one.

16.2 Emails
16.2.1 Reebok, USA to Sportarena, Germany

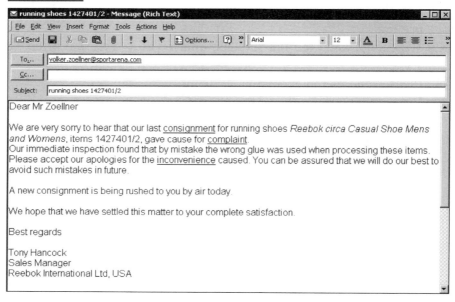

16.2.2 Twinings, UK to Broken English Berlin, Germany

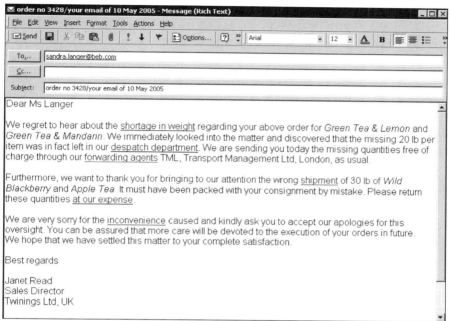

16.3 Text components

DC1 We regret to hear that our last consignment gave cause for complaint. We immediately looked into the matter and realised that the wrong items were sent to you by mistake. Please return the goods at our expense for an exchange for the correct items.

> *Wir bedauern zu erfahren, dass unsere letzte Sendung Anlass zur Beschwerde gab. Wir haben uns sofort der Sache angenommen und festgestellt, dass Ihnen versehentlich die falschen Artikel zugesandt wurden. Bitte senden Sie uns die Waren auf unsere Kosten zurück, damit wir diese gegen die richtigen Artikel austauschen können.*

DC2 We are sorry to hear that our last delivery did not turn out to your satisfaction. Our inspections found that the wrong material was used for your order.
Please return the goods at our expense. A new delivery will be send to you next week. You can be assured that we will do our best to avoid such mistakes in future.

> *Wir bedauern, dass Sie mit unserer letzten Lieferung nicht zufrieden waren. Unsere Prüfung ergab, dass versehentlich das falsche Material für Ihren Auftrag verwendet wurde.*
> *Bitte senden Sie die Waren auf unsere Kosten zurück. Wir werden Ihnen nächste Woche eine neue Lieferung zusenden.*
> *Wir versichern Ihnen, dass wir unser Bestes tun werden, um derartige Fehler in Zukunft zu vermeiden.*

DC3 Thank you for sending us samples of the faulty tennis shoes. Our inspection found a manufacturing error. Replacements will be shipped to you free of charge today.
We hope that we have settled this matter to your complete satisfaction.

> *Vielen Dank für die Zusendung von Mustern der mangelhaften Tennisschuhe. Unsere Prüfung ergab, dass hier ein Produktionsfehler vorliegt. Kostenloser Ersatz wird Ihnen noch heute zugesandt.*
> *Wir hoffen, die Angelegenheit hiermit zu Ihrer vollen Zufriedenheit geregelt zu haben.*

DC4 We are sorry to hear that the last consignment did not reach you safely. It was in good condition when handed over to the shipping company, as you will see from the clean B/L. We suppose that the damage has occurred in transit. Therefore, we cannot assume any liability in this case. Please enter a claim with your insurance company.

Wir bedauern zu erfahren, dass die letzte Sendung nicht wohlbehalten bei Ihnen angekommen ist. Bei Übergabe an die Reederei war sie in einwandfreiem Zustand, wie Sie dem reinen Konnossement entnehmen können. Wir nehmen an, dass die Beschädigung sich auf dem Transportweg ereignet hat. Aus diesem Grunde können wir in diesem Falle keine Haftung übernehmen. Bitte melden Sie den Schaden bei Ihrer Versicherungsgesellschaft.

DC5   We refer to your complaint about the quality of our tennis shoes. However, after careful inspection of the samples you returned to us, a fault in the material could not be found. Therefore, we have to inform you that your claim is not justified and that we cannot accept the return of the consignment. We regret not being able to give you a more positive reply.

Wir beziehen uns auf Ihre Beschwerde über die Qualität unserer Tennisschuhe. Nach sorgfältiger Prüfung der von Ihnen zurückgesandten Muster können wir jedoch keinen Materialfehler feststellen. Daher müssen wir Ihnen mitteilen, dass Ihre Beschwerde nicht berechtigt ist und dass wir die Sendung nicht zurücknehmen können. Wir bedauern, Ihnen keinen positiveren Bescheid geben zu können.

DC6   We refer to your complaint about the quality of our tennis shoes. Although we cannot find a fault on our part in this matter, we will send you replacements free of charge as a gesture of goodwill.

Wir beziehen uns auf Ihre Beschwerde über die Qualität unserer Tennisschuhe. Obwohl wir in diesem Fall keinen Fehler unsererseits feststellen können, senden wir Ihnen aus Kulanz kostenlosen Ersatz zu.

16.4 Tasks

Please deal with <u>complaints</u> by email using the following details and make use of the text components wherever you can:

16.4.1 Microsoft Corp, USA to Saturn, Germany

- Betreff/Anrede
- Sie haben soeben die Nachricht bekommen, dass die letzte Sendung Software *Windows XP* nicht vollständig beim Kunden angekommen ist.
- Sie bedauern zu hören, dass nur 4 der 5 gelieferten Paletten in Köln angekommen sind.
- Ihre Nachforschungen bei der Fluggesellschaft haben ergeben, dass eine Palette am Flughafen in New York stehen geblieben ist.
- Die fehlende Palette mit den 200 Stück Software *Windows XP* wird noch heute mit dem nächsten Flugzeug nachgeliefert.
- Sie bitten die entstandenen Unannehmlichkeiten zu entschuldigen, auf die Sie aber keinen Einfluss hatten.
- Sie hoffen, dass die fehlende Palette in einwandfreiem Zustand in Köln ankommt.
- Schlusssatz

16.4.2 Durable, Germany to Office Supplies, Saudi Arabia

- Betreff/Anrede
- Sie bedauern zu hören, dass die Klarsichthüllen nicht in einwandfreiem Zustand beim Kunden angekommen sind.
- Sie versichern, dass die Ware vor Versand sorgfältig von der Qualitätskontrolle geprüft wurde und in einwandfreiem Zustand war, als sie dem Spediteur übergeben wurde.
- Sie nehmen daher an, dass sich die Beschädigung im Hafen oder auf dem Transportweg ereignet hat.
- Möglicherweise ist die Ladung unsachgemäß behandelt worden.
- Unter diesen Umständen können Sie nicht für die Beschädigung der Ware verantwortlich gemacht werden.

- Sie bitten den Kunden, den Schaden umgehend seiner Transportversicherung zu melden, die für den Schaden haftet.
- Sie werden dem Kunden innerhalb der nächsten 10 Tage eine Ersatzlieferung zuschicken, die Sie allerdings nicht kostenlos vornehmen können.
- Aus Kulanz bieten Sie dem Kunden aber gerne ein Zahlungsziel von 3 Monaten an.
- Schlusssatz

16.4.3 Fill in the missing prepositions

1. ... mistake the wrong items were sent to you.
2. Thank you ... sending us samples ... the faulty goods.
3. The consignment was ... good condition when handed over ... the shipping company, as you will see ... the clean on-board B/L.
4. ... these circumstances, we cannot accept the return ... the consignment.
5. Please enter a claim ... the shipping company.
6. Please return the goods ... our expense.
7. Although we cannot find a fault ... our part ... this matter, we will send you replacements free of charge ... a gesture ... goodwill.
8. ... reply ...you email ... 2 May we have to point out that according ... the terms of delivery agreed ..., we cannot assume any liability ... this case.
9. The damage must have occurred ... transit.
10. Although the guarantee period has already expired, we are willing to repair the scanners ... free.

UNIT 17 SENDING A PAYMENT REMINDER

17.1 Key facts

Sending a <u>payment reminder</u> demands sensitiveness. Reminders can affect business relations negatively if they are expressed too strongly or too early. Therefore, in foreign trade, the export department of a company is often consulted when reminding its customers to <u>effect payment</u> if they failed to pay within the credit period agreed upon. The export team knows its customers and their <u>payment behaviour</u> very well and should be contacted first in order to decide how best to proceed.

Depending on the philosophy of a company three or four reminders are sent by mail before the matter is placed in the hands of the seller's <u>solicitors</u> or a <u>collection agency</u>. Should the debtor nevertheless ignore the repeated requests and final demand for payment from a lawyer, eventually, legal action will be taken.

If the buyer simply overlooked payment, he will apologise and pay the amount overdue. In case of financial difficulties, however, he will <u>ask for extension</u>. Generally, the seller will be prepared to grant a <u>respite</u> if the customer has always met his obligations promptly.

17.2 Letters

17.2.1 Reebok, USA to Sportarena, Germany

Reebok

Reebok International Ltd
1895 J W Foster Boulevard
Canton, MA 02021 USA
Phone: 1-800-934-3566 Fax: 1-800-934-3455
Internet: www.reebok.com

JB/ac

July 23, 2005

Sportarena
Neumarkt 10
50969 Koeln
Germany

Reminder

Ladies and Gentlemen

We regret to inform you that the <u>due amount</u> mentioned below still
remains <u>outstanding for payment</u>.

Invoice no 23889 of June 23, 2005 for US$5,450.00

Thank you in advance for your prompt attention to this matter.
If you have already forwarded your payment, please disregard this letter.

Sincerely

Jim Brown
Accounting
Reebok International Ltd, USA

17.2.2 Twinings, UK to Broken English Berlin, Germany

South Way Andover Hampshire SP105AQ Great Britain
Telephone: + 44 (0) 1264 334477   Fax: + 44 (0) 1264 335577
Internet: www.twinings.com

SW/ac

5 September 2005

Broken English
Koertestr, 10
10967 Berlin
Germany

Dear Sir/Madam

SECOND REMINDER

We kindly ask you for immediate payment of the <u>due amount</u> to one of
our accounts. Despite a previous reminder, the amount mentioned below
still remains <u>outstanding for payment</u>:

<u>Invoice</u> no 2367 dated 8 July 2005 for € 2,599.50
due on 8 August 2005
First reminder dated 22 August 2005

Please remit the amount immediately or give us a call to discuss this
matter.
If you have already forwarded your payment, please disregard this letter.

Yours faithfully

Sarah Winter
Accounting

17.3 Text components

PR1 This is to inform you that we still have not received payment of the invoice mentioned below:

Invoice no 2367 dated 8 July 2005 for €2,000.00 due on 8 August 2005

Thank you in advance for your prompt attention to this matter.

If you have already forwarded your payment, please disregard this letter.

> *Hiermit teilen wir Ihnen mit, dass die unten aufgeführte Rechnung noch nicht beglichen wurde:*
> **Rechnung Nr. 2367 vom 8. Juli 2005 über € 2.599,50, fällig am 8. August 2005.**
> *Vielen Dank im Voraus für Ihre umgehende Bearbeitung.*
> *Sollte die Zahlung zwischenzeitlich erfolgt sein, so betrachten Sie dieses Schreiben bitte als gegenstandslos.*

PR2 Despite a previous reminder, the amount mentioned below still remains outstanding for payment:

Invoice no 2367 dated 8 July 2005 for €2,000.00 due on 8 August 2005

First reminder dated 22 August 2005

Please remit the amount immediately or give us a call to discuss the matter.

If you have already forwarded your payment, please disregard this letter.

> *Wir bedauern feststellen zu müssen, dass der unten aufgeführte Betrag trotz vorheriger Zahlungserinnerung noch zur Zahlung aussteht:*
> **Rechnung Nr. 2367 vom 8. Juli 2005 über € 2.599,50, fällig am 8. August 2005**
> **1. Mahnung vom 22. August 2005**
> *Bitte überweisen Sie den Betrag unverzüglich oder rufen Sie uns an, um die Angelegenheit zu besprechen.*

Sollte die Zahlung zwischenzeitlich erfolgt sein, so betrachten Sie dieses Schreiben bitte als gegenstandslos.

PR3   We have not received any answer to our previous reminders regarding the invoice mentioned below. We regret to inform you that no further products will be despatched until we have received your remittance.
Invoice no 2367 dated 8 July 2005 for €2,000.00 due on 8 August 2005
First reminder dated 22 August 2005
Second reminder dated 5 September 2005
We look forward to receiving your prompt remittance.
If you have already forwarded your payment, please disregard this letter.

Wir haben bisher noch keine Antwort auf unsere mehrfachen Mahnungen auf die unten aufgeführte Rechnung erhalten. Wir bedauern, Ihnen mitteilen zu müssen, dass keine weiteren Produkte an Sie versendet werden, bis wir Ihre Überweisung erhalten haben.
Rechnung Nr. 2367 vom 8. Juli 2005 über € 2.599,50, fällig am 8. August 2005
1. Mahnung vom 22. August 2005
2. Mahnung vom 5. September 2005
Vielen Dank für Ihre umgehende Überweisung.
Sollte die Zahlung zwischenzeitlich erfolgt sein, so betrachten Sie dieses Schreiben bitte als gegenstandslos.

PR4   Despite previous reminders, we are still not in receipt of your payment referring to the invoice mentioned below. Your account is now seriously overdue, and we must inform you that if payment in full is not received within the next ten days, your account will be passed over for legal action:
Invoice no 2367 dated 8 July 2005 for €2,000.00 due on 8 August 2005

First reminder dated 22 August 2005
Second reminder dated 5 September 2 004
Third reminder dated 19 September 2005
We look forward to receiving your prompt remittance. If you have already forwarded your payment, please disregard this letter.

> *Trotz mehrfacher Mahnungen ist die Zahlung der unten aufgeführten Rechnung noch nicht bei uns eingegangen. Der Rechnungsbetrag ist nun längst überfällig und wir müssen Sie darauf aufmerksam machen, dass wir rechtliche Schritte einleiten werden, wenn die Zahlung des vollen Rechnungsbetrages nicht innerhalb der nächsten zehn Tage bei uns eingeht:*
> **Rechnung Nr. 2367 vom 8. Juli 2005 über € 2.599,50, fällig am 8. August 2005**
> **1. Mahnung vom 22. August 2005**
> **2. Mahnung vom 5. September 2005**
> **3. Mahnung vom 19. September 2005**
> *Vielen Dank für Ihre umgehende Überweisung.*
> *Sollte die Zahlung zwischenzeitlich erfolgt sein, so betrachten Sie dieses Schreiben bitte als gegenstandslos.*

PR5 Despite previous reminders, we are still not in receipt of your payment referring to the invoice mentioned below. Your account is now seriously overdue, and we must inform you that if payment in full is not received within the next ten days, your account will be recovered through a debt collection agency[10]:
Invoice no 2367 dated 8 July 2005 for €2,000.00 due on 8 August 2005
First reminder dated 22 August 2005
Second reminder dated 5 September 2005
Third reminder dated 19 September 2005
We look forward to receiving your prompt remittance. If you have already forwarded your payment, please disregard this letter.

---

[10] When a past-due invoice becomes an issue, debt collection agencies provide collection tools to recover the money of debtors.

Trotz mehrfacher Mahnungen ist die Zahlung der unten aufgeführten Rechnung noch nicht bei uns eingegangen. Der Rechnungsbetrag ist nun längst überfällig und wir müssen Sie darauf aufmerksam machen, dass wir den Betrag durch ein Inkassoinstitut eintreiben lassen, wenn die Zahlung des vollen Rechnungsbetrages nicht innerhalb der nächsten zehn Tage bei uns eingeht:
Rechnung Nr. 2367 vom 8. Juli 2005 über € 2.599,50, fällig am 8. August 2005
1. Mahnung vom 22. August 2005
2. Mahnung vom 5. September 2005
3. Mahnung vom 19. September 2005
Vielen Dank für Ihre umgehende Überweisung.
Sollte die Zahlung zwischenzeitlich erfolgt sein, so betrachten Sie dieses Schreiben bitte als gegenstandslos.

PR6   Despite previous reminders, we are still not in receipt of your payment of the invoice mentioned below. Your account is now seriously overdue, and we must inform you that if payment in full is not received within the next ten days, we will have no alternative but to place the matter in the hands of our solicitors.
Invoice no 2367 dated 8 July 2005 for €2,000.00 due on 8 August 2005
First reminder dated 22 August 2005
Second reminder dated 5 September 2005
Third reminder dated 19 September 2005
We look forward to receiving your prompt remittance.
If you have already forwarded your payment, please disregard this letter.

Trotz mehrfacher Mahnungen ist die Zahlung der unten aufgeführten Rechnung noch nicht bei uns eingegangen. Der Rechnungsbetrag ist nun längst überfällig und wir müssen Sie darauf aufmerksam machen, dass wir die Sache unseren Anwälten übergeben werden, wenn die

Zahlung des vollen Rechnungsbetrages nicht innerhalb der nächsten zehn Tage bei uns eingeht.
Rechnung Nr. 2367 vom 8. Juli 2005 über € 2.599,50, fällig am 8. August 2005
1. Mahnung vom 22. August 2005
2. Mahnung vom 5. September 2005
3. Mahnung vom 19. September 2005
Vielen Dank für Ihre umgehende Überweisung.
Sollte die Zahlung zwischenzeitlich erfolgt sein, so betrachten Sie dieses Schreiben bitte als gegenstandslos.

PR7 This is to inform you that we have instructed our bankers today to settle your invoice no 2334 of 10 May 2005 for the amount of €2,500. Please accept our apologies for the delay but your invoice was overlooked in the pressure of business.

> *Hiermit teilen wir Ihnen mit, dass wir heute unsere Bank angewiesen haben, Ihre Rechnung Nr. 2334 vom 10. Mai 2005 über einen Betrag von € 2.500,- zu begleichen. Bitte entschuldigen Sie die Verspätung, aber Ihre Rechnung wurde im Geschäftsalltag übersehen.*

PR8 Due to the bankruptcy of one of our key customers, we are experiencing temporary financial difficulties. In view of our good payment behaviour in the past we would be grateful if you could grant us a respite of 30 days.

> *Der Konkurs eines unserer Hauptkunden hat uns temporär in Zahlungsschwierigkeiten gebracht. Angesichts unserer guten Zahlungsmoral in der Vergangenheit, wären wir Ihnen sehr dankbar, wenn Sie uns einen Zahlungsaufschub von 30 Tagen gewähren würden.*

17.4 Tasks

Please send <u>payment reminders</u> by **letter** using the following details and make use of the text components wherever you can:

17.4.1 Microsoft Corp, USA to Saturn, Germany

- Betreff/Anrede
- Sie bedauern mitteilen zu müssen, dass trotz Ihrer Zahlungserinnerung vom 14. Januar 2005 die Rechnung Nr. 245/54 vom 02. Dezember 2005 über einen Betrag von US$ 4.500,- noch nicht beglichen wurde.
- Sollte der Kunde irgendwelche Zahlungsschwierigkeiten haben, bitten Sie um umgehende Mitteilung.
- Ansonsten ist die obige Rechnung nun ohne weiteren Verzug innerhalb der nächsten Tage zu begleichen.
- Sollte der Betrag inzwischen bezahlt worden sein, so ist dieses Schreiben als gegenstandslos zu betrachten.
- Schlusssatz

17.4.2 Office Supplies, Saudi Arabia to Durable, Germany

- Betreff/Anrede
- Sie haben die Zahlungserinnerung vom 25. März 2005 über einen Betrag von US$ 3.250,- erhalten und entschuldigen sich für den Zahlungsverzug.
- Da z.Zt. die Zahlungen Ihrer Kunden sehr schleppend eingehen, bitten Sie um einen Zahlungsaufschub bis Ende April dieses Jahres.
- Sie versichern, den vollen Betrag bis zu diesem Stichtag zu begleichen.
- Sie danken im voraus für das Verständnis.
- Schlusssatz

17.4.3 Fill in the missing prepositions

1. We regret to inform you that our invoice no 2334 ... 10 May 2005 ...the amount ... €2,500 is still overdue.
2. The amount mentioned below still remains outstanding ... payment.
3. If payment is not received ... 12 July 2005, we will have no alternative but to place the matter ... the hands ... our solicitors.
4. Unless payment is received ... 2 May 2005, we will have the amount collected ... a collection agency.
5. Despite previous reminders, we are still not ... receipt ... your payment ... the outstanding amount mentioned below.
6. We must inform you that if payment ... full is not received ... the next ten days, your account will be passed ... ... legal action.
7. Thank you ... advance ... your prompt attention ... this matter.
8. We regret to inform you that no further products will be despatched ... we have received your remittance.
9. Please accept our apologies ... the delay but your invoice was overlooked ... the pressure ... business.
10. ... view ... our good payment behaviour ... the past we would be grateful if you could grant us an extension ... 60 days.

UNIT 18   DEALING WITH FAIRS

18.1 Key facts

If companies <u>exhibit</u> at fairs, they will inform their customers in good time. Fair details are provided on the Internet and customers are often invited for evening events with the companies exhibiting.

After a successful fair <u>follow-up letters</u> are sent to the customers and contacts thanking them for visiting the company's stand and sending them the brochures, leaflets, catalogues, price list or <u>quotations</u> requested.

> There is a general difference between exhibition, exposition and fair.
>
> **Exhibition:** a collection of pictures, sculptures, etc for public viewing.
>
> **Exposition:** an exhibition in which goods, works of art, etc are shown to the public.
>
> **Fair:** an exhibition where manufacturers show products that they want to sell to people from other industries.

18.2 Emails
18.2.1 Reebok, USA to Sportarena, Germany

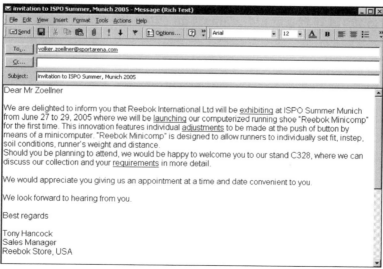

18.2.2 Twinings, UK to Broken English Berlin, Germany

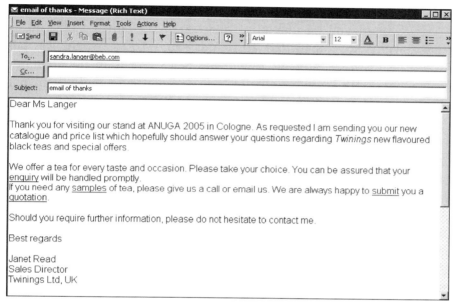

Dear Ms Langer

Thank you for visiting our stand at ANUGA 2005 in Cologne. As requested I am sending you our new catalogue and price list which hopefully should answer your questions regarding *Twinings* new flavoured black teas and special offers.

We offer a tea for every taste and occasion. Please take your choice. You can be assured that your enquiry will be handled promptly.
If you need any samples of tea, please give us a call or email us. We are always happy to submit you a quotation.

Should you require further information, please do not hesitate to contact me.

Best regards

Janet Read
Sales Director
Twinings Ltd, UK

18.3 Text components

TF1   We are pleased to inform you that NIKE will be participating at *ISPO* Winter Munich from January 31 to February 3, 2005. We will be located in hall 26, at stand C329. We look forward to meeting you and discussing our cooperation in Germany. **(AE)**

> *Wir freuen uns, Ihnen mitzuteilen, dass NIKE an der ISPO Winter München vom 31.01. - 03.02.2005 als Aussteller teilnimmt. Sie finden uns in Halle 26, Stand C329.*
>
> *Wir würden uns freuen, Sie zu treffen und unsere Zusammenarbeit in Deutschland mit Ihnen zu besprechen.*

TF2 We are delighted to inform you that Hewlett-Packard will be exhibiting at *CeBIT* Hanover from March 18 to 24, 2005 where we will be launching our *hp star* pocket notebook for the first time.

Should you be planning to attend, we would be pleased to welcome you in hall 10 to our stand C328, where we can discuss our product range and your requirements in more detail. We would appreciate you giving us an appointment at a time and date convenient to you. **(AE)**

> *Wir freuen uns sehr, Ihnen mitzuteilen, dass Hewlett-Packard auf der CeBIT in Hannover vom 18.-24. 03.2005 ausstellen wird, wo wir erstmals unser Pocket-Notebook hp star vorstellen werden.*
>
> *Wenn Sie einen Messebesuch geplant haben, würden wir uns freuen, Sie in Halle 10, auf unserem Stand C328 zu begrüßen und mit Ihnen unsere Produktpalette und Ihren Bedarf ausführlich zu besprechen. Bitte teilen Sie uns mit, welcher Tag und welche Uhrzeit Ihnen angenehm ist.*

TF3 We would like to give our clients and contacts the opportunity to see several hardware solutions that will be on display during the *CeBIT* from March 18 to 24, 2005. We will organize 30 minutes tours from 10am to 4 pm every day in groups of two to ten. If you would like to join us for a tour, please contact us by email. **(AE)**

> *Wir würden unseren Kunden und Geschäftspartnern gerne die Möglichkeit geben, mehrere Hardware-Lösungen kennen zu lernen, die wir auf der CeBIT vom 18.-24. März 2005 ausstellen. Wir werden an allen Tagen 30-minütige Führungen von 10.00-16.00 Uhr in Gruppen von 4-10 Personen durchführen. Wenn Sie Interesse an einer Führung haben, so kontaktieren Sie uns bitte per E-Mail.*

TF4   We are pleased to invite you to a typical Bavarian evening at *Franziskaner Brauhaus* in Munich on Monday 27 June 2005. Attached you will find our invitation. Please send us your confirmation asap and let us know how many persons are going to attend.

> *Wir würden Sie gerne am Montag, den 27. Juni 2005 zu einem typischen Bayrischen Abend im Franziskaner Brauhaus in München einladen. Als Dateianhang senden wir Ihnen unsere Einladung. Bitte senden Sie uns Ihre Bestätigung schnellstmöglich zu und teilen Sie uns mit, wie viele Personen teilnehmen werden.*

TF5   We would like to invite you to a private dinner on Monday 29 November 2005 at *Arabella Airport Hotel* in Frankfurt. If this date is convenient for you, please send us your confirmation by 15 October 2005.

> *Wir würden Sie gerne zu einem Abendessen am Montag, den 29. November 2005 im Arabella Airport Hotel in Frankfurt einladen. Wenn Ihnen dieser Termin zusagt, bitten wir um Ihre Zusage bis zum 15. Oktober 2005.*

TF6   Thank you for visiting our stand at the *CeBIT* in Hanover. As requested, I am sending you our novelty catalogue including price list, which hopefully should answer your questions regarding our innovations and special offers.

> Should you have any further questions please do not hesitate to contact me.

> *Vielen Dank für Ihren Besuch an unseren Stand auf der CeBIT in Hannover. Wunschgemäß senden wir Ihnen unseren Neuheiten-Katalog inklusive Preisliste, der Ihnen sicherlich Ihre Fragen bezüglich unserer Innovationen und Sonderangebote beantworten wird. Sollten Sie noch Fragen haben, so können Sie sich jederzeit an mich wenden.*

TF7 I refer to our conversation at ANUGA in Cologne and thank you once again for your special interest in our green teas. If you need any samples, please give us a call. We are always happy to submit you a quotation.

Please have a look at our website: www.twinings.com or email your enquiries to janet.read@twinings.com.

Ich komme zurück auf unser Gespräch auf der ANUGA in Köln und möchte mich nochmals bei Ihnen für Ihr besonderes Interesse an unseren Grüntees bedanken. Wenn Sie Muster benötigen, so rufen Sie uns bitte an. Wir sind jederzeit gerne bereit, Ihnen ein Angebot zu unterbreiten. Bitte schauen Sie auf unsere Website www.twinings.com *oder schicken Sie uns Ihre Anfragen per E-Mail an* janet.read@twinings.com.

18.4 Tasks

Please write emails using the following details and make use of the text components wherever you can:

18.4.1 Microsoft Corp, USA to Saturn, Germany

- Betreff/Anrede
- Sie teilen mit, dass Sie auf der *CeBIT* in Hannover vom 18.-24. März 2005 ausstellen.
- Sie sind in Halle 3, Stand C329.
- Sie bieten während der Messetage ein abwechslungsreiches Programm mit vielen Gewinnspielen und Führungen durch „*Die Welt der Software*" mit Microsoft Corp.
- Diese 45-minütigen Führungen finden an allen Tagen von 10.00 – 16.00 Uhr statt.
- Sie bitten um Anmeldung bis zum 1.Februar 2005 per E-Mail.
- Einen Terminvorschlag mit Datum und Uhrzeit auf der Messe würden Sie begrüßen.
- Sie würden sich freuen, den Kunden zu treffen, um die weitere Zusammenarbeit mit ihm zu besprechen.
- Schlusssatz

18.4.2 Durable, Germany to Office Supplies, Saudi Arabia

*   Betreff/Anrede
*   Sie danken dem Kunden für den Messebesuch auf der *Paperworld* in Frankfurt und das Interesse an Ihren Produkten.
*   Ihr Motto war dieses Jahr „*The key to success*", passend zu den neuen Schlüsselkästen die Sie erstmals auf der Messe vorgestellt haben.
*   Wunschgemäß senden Sie dem Kunden Ihren Katalog sowie Broschüren über Ihre neuen Schlüsselkästen.
*   Als einer der führenden Hersteller von Bürobedarf bieten Sie klassische Produkte wie Mappen und Hefter, aber auch Artikel zur Schreibtisch- und EDV-Organisation sowie Ordnungssysteme an.
*   Sollte der Kunde Muster benötigen, so bitten Sie um Mitteilung.
*   Sie würden sich freuen, ihm ein detailliertes Angebot zu unterbreiten und bitten um Angabe der ungefähren Liefermengen.
*   Sollte der Kunde noch weitere Fragen haben, so kann er sich jederzeit gerne an Sie wenden.
*   Schlusssatz

18.4.3 Fill in the missing prepositions

1. We are pleased to inform you that NIKE will be participating ... *ISPO* Munich ... January 31 to February 3, 2005.
2. We will be located ... hall 26, ... stand C329.
3. Should you be planning to attend, we would be pleased to welcome you ... our stand C328, where we can discuss our product range and your requirements ... more detail.
4. We would appreciate you giving us an appointment ... a time and date convenient ... you.
5. We would like to give our clients and contacts the opportunity to see several hardware solutions, which will be ... display, ... the *CeBIT*.

6. We will organise 30 minutes tours ... 10am ... 4 pm every day ... groups ... two ... eight.

7. If you would like to join us ... a tour, please contact us ... email.

8. Attached please find an invitation ... a private dinner ... Hewlett-Packard ... Monday November 29, 2005 ... *Arabella Airport Hotel* ... Frankfurt.

9. Please confirm your participation ... February 15, 2005 and let us know how many persons are going to attend.

10. Thank you ... visiting our stand ... *CeBIT* ... Hanover.

UNIT 19 TRAVELLING ON BUSINESS

19.1 Key facts

If manufacturers go on business trips they generally want to renew or intensify business relations or establish new contacts.

Arrangements such as booking of flights or hotels have to be made in good time. Additionally, you have to check if your visit is convenient.

After a business trip emails of thanks should follow and suggestions and topics discussed must be acted upon.

19.2 Emails

19.2.1 Reebok, USA to Sportarena, Germany

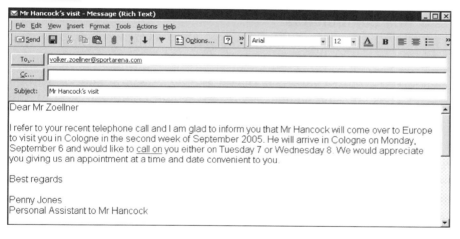

19.2.2 Reebok, USA to Sportarena, Germany

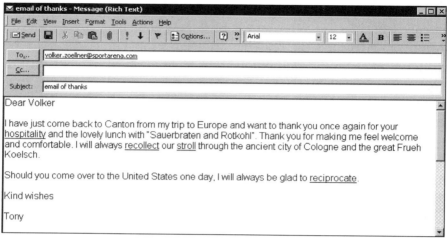

Dear Volker

I have just come back to Canton from my trip to Europe and want to thank you once again for your hospitality and the lovely lunch with "Sauerbraten and Rotkohl". Thank you for making me feel welcome and comfortable. I will always recollect our stroll through the ancient city of Cologne and the great Frueh Koelsch.

Should you come over to the United States one day, I will always be glad to reciprocate.

Kind wishes

Tony

19.3 Text components

TB1 We are glad to inform you that Mr Miller is going to visit you at the beginning of November. He will arrive on Monday 1 November 2005, in Berlin so that he could call on you on Tuesday 2 or Wednesday 3. We would appreciate you giving us an appointment at a time and date convenient to you.

> *Wir freuen uns, Ihnen mitzuteilen, dass Herr Miller Sie Anfang März besuchen wird. Er kommt am Montag, den 1. November 2005 in Berlin an, so dass er Sie am Dienstag, den 2. März oder Mittwoch, den 3. November treffen könnte. Bitte teilen Sie uns mit, an welchem Tag und zu welcher Uhrzeit Ihnen ein Termin zusagt.*

TB2 We refer to your email of today and are pleased to inform you that an appointment on Wednesday 3 November 2005 at 10 am would be convenient. We look forward to your early confirmation.

> *Wir beziehen uns auf Ihre E-Mail von heute und freuen uns, Ihnen mitzuteilen, dass uns ein Termin am Mittwoch, den 3. November 2005, um 10.00 Uhr,*

angenehm wäre. Über Ihre baldige Bestätigung würden wir uns freuen.

TB3 This is to confirm that Mr Miller will call on Mr Schmidt on Wednesday 3 November 2005, at 10 am.

> *Hiermit bestätigen wir den Termin der Herren Miller und Schmidt für Mittwoch, den 3. November 2005, um 10.00 Uhr.*

TB4 Please let us have your flight details so that we can arrange for someone to pick you up from the airport.
Should you require any hotel reservation please let us know.

> *Bitte teilen Sie uns Ihre Flugdaten mit, damit wir Sie vom Flughafen abholen lassen können.*
> *Wenn wir eine Hotelreservierung für Sie vornehmen sollen, so geben Sie uns bitte Bescheid.*

TB5 We would like to invite you to be our guest for dinner on any day convenient to you during your stay in Cologne. Thank you for your prompt reply.

> *Wir würden uns sehr freuen, wenn wir Sie während Ihres Aufenthaltes in Köln an einem Tag Ihrer Wahl zum Abendessen einladen dürfen. Vielen Dank für Ihre baldige Antwort.*

TB6 Thank you very much for your invitation for dinner, which I gladly accept for Wednesday 3 November 2005, following our appointment.

> *Vielen Dank für Ihre Einladung zum Abendessen, die ich gerne für Mittwoch, den 3. November 2005, im Anschluss an unseren Termin, annehme.*

TB7 Thank you very much for your invitation for dinner on Wednesday 3 November 2005.
Unfortunately, I am unable to accept, as my diary is heavily committed at that time.

> *Vielen Dank für Ihre Einladung zum Abendessen für Mittwoch, den 3. November 2005. Leider kann ich diese nicht wahrnehmen, da ich zu der Zeit bereits anderweitige Verpflichtungen habe.*

TB8 I have just returned from my trip to Europe and want to thank you very much for your hospitality and the lovely dinner with "Schweinebraten und Knoedel" in Munich. Thank you for making me feel welcome and comfortable. I will always recollect the enjoyable evening in the "Hofbraeuhaus" and the great Munich beer.
Should you come over to the United States one day, I will always be glad to reciprocate.

> *Ich bin gerade von meiner Europareise zurück gekehrt und möchte mich herzlich für Ihre Gastfreundschaft und das leckere Abendessen in München mit Schweinebraten und Knödel bedanken. Danke, dass Sie dafür gesorgt haben, dass ich mich wohl gefühlt habe. Ich werde mich immer gerne an den schönen Abend im Hofbräuhaus und das gute Münchner Bier zurück erinnern.*

> *Sollten Sie einmal in die USA kommen, so würde ich mich freuen, mich für Ihre Gastfreundschaft revanchieren zu können.*

TB9 I am out of the office until 17 October 2005. I will be happy to answer your emails asap on my return. Thanks for your understanding. If you need urgent assistance, please contact our customer service team, phone: …, email: …

> *Ich bin bis zum 17. Oktober 2005 nicht im Büro. Ich werde Ihre E-Mails nach meiner Rückkehr schnellstmöglich beantworten. Vielen Dank für Ihr Verständnis.*

> *In dringenden Fällen wenden Sie sich bitte an unseren Kundenservice. Tel.: …, E-Mail:..*

19.4 Tasks

Please write emails using the following details and make use of the text components wherever you can:

19.4.1 Microsoft Corp, USA to Saturn, Germany

- Betreff/Anrede
- Der Verkaufsleiter von Microsoft Corp, Herr Scott, plant in der 2. Oktoberwoche 2005 eine Europareise und würde bei dieser Gelegenheit gerne den Leiter der Einkaufsabteilung von Saturn, Herrn Neumann, persönlich kennen lernen, um mit ihm die weitere Zusammenarbeit für 2005 zu besprechen.
- Herr Scott kommt am Dienstag, den 11. Oktober 2005 in Köln an und könnte somit am 12., 13. oder 14. Oktober einen Termin bei Saturn wahrnehmen.
- Herr Scott bittet um Mitteilung, welches Datum und welche Uhrzeit sich am besten einrichten lässt.
- Schlusssatz

19.4.2 Office Supplies, Saudi Arabia to Durable, Germany

- Betreff/Anrede
- Der Einkäufer von Office Supplies, Herr Said, ist gestern wieder in Djidda angekommen und möchte sich bei dem Verkaufsleiter von Durable, Herrn Berger, herzlich für die ihm beim Besuch in Iserlohn erwiesene Gastfreundschaft bedanken.
- Er hat sich in dem Hotel „Seilersee", welches Durable für ihn reserviert hat, sehr wohl gefühlt.
- Er wird immer wieder gerne an das gemeinsame deutsche Abendessen im „Haus Seilersee" und an die nette deutsche Atmosphäre zurückdenken.
- Herr Said wird die besprochene Auftragsplanung für das kommende Geschäftsjahr zu den ausgehandelten Konditionen noch im Laufe dieser Woche mit der Geschäftsführung besprechen und Herrn Berger dann entsprechend benachrichtigen.

- Sollte sich die Gelegenheit bieten, dass Herr Berger nach Saudi Arabien kommt, so würde sich Herr Said sehr freuen, die Gastfreundschaft zu erwidern.
- Schlusssatz

19.4.3 Fill in the missing prepositions

1. Mr Miller will arrive ... Monday 1 November 2005, so that he could call ... you ... Tuesday 2 or Wednesday 3.
2. We would appreciate you giving us an appointment ... a time and date convenient ... you.
3. This is to confirm that Mr Hancock will call ... Mr Zöllner ... Wednesday
   November, 3 ... 10 am.
4. Please let us have your flight details enabling us to arrange ... someone to pick you ... ... the airport.
5. We would like to invite you to be our guest ... lunch ... any day convenient ... you during your stay ... Cologne.
6. Thank you very much for your invitation ... lunch, which I gladly accept.
7. Unfortunately, I cannot accept your kind invitation, as my diary is heavily committed ... that time.
8. I have just returned ... my trip ... Europe and want to thank you very much ... your hospitality.
9. If there is an opportunity ... us to reciprocate, please let us know.
10. I am out of the office ... 17 October 2005. I will be happy to answer your emails asap ... my return.

UNIT 20   WRITING MISCELLANEOUS CORRESPONDENCE

20.1 Key facts

In everyday business life you will have to cope with various matters. Below you will find a choice of special situations you should be able to handle by post or email.
- Changes in personnel
- Retirement
- Appointment to a new job
- Anniversary
- New representative/subsidiary
- Directions
- Condolence

20.2 Emails
20.2.1 Reebok, USA to Sportarena, Germany

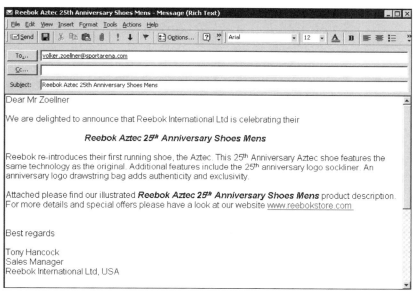

20.2.2 Broken English Berlin, Germany to Twinings, UK

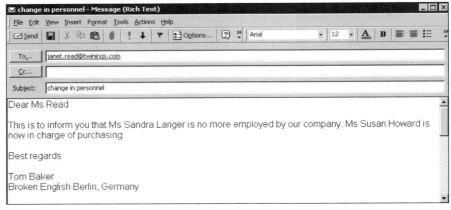

20.3 Text components

MC1 This is to inform you that Mr Miller is retiring at the end of October this year. His successor will be Jim Brown.

> *Hiermit möchten wir Ihnen mitteilen, dass Herr Miller Ende Oktober dieses Jahres in den Ruhestand geht. Sein Nachfolger wird Jim Brown.*

MC2 Congratulations for being appointed to the Purchasing Manager of Hewlett-Packard. We wish you every success in your new position.

> *Zu Ihrer Beförderung als Einkaufsleiter von Hewlett-Packard möchten wir Ihnen herzlich gratulieren. Wir wünschen Ihnen alles Gute für Ihre neue Position.*

MC3 Thank you for your email of today asking for the way to our company. A site map and detailed directions will be found at www.twinings.com.
Should you have any further questions, please do not hesitate to contact me.

> *Vielen Dank für Ihre E-Mail von heute mit der Bitte um eine Wegbeschreibung zu unserer Firma. Wir möchten*

Sie darauf aufmerksam machen, dass Sie unter www. twinings.com eine Standortkarte und eine ausführliche Wegbeschreibung finden.
Sollte Sie noch Fragen haben, so können Sie sich gerne an mich wenden.

MC4 This is to inform you that Ms Jones is no more employed by our company. Ms Hall is now in charge of customer support.

> *Hiermit möchten wir Ihnen mitteilen, dass Frau Jones nicht mehr bei uns im Unternehmen tätig ist. Frau Hall ist jetzt zuständig für die Gästebetreuung.*

MC5 We are pleased to inform you that we have recently opened a new subsidiary in Moscow, Russia. For enquiries please contact Ms Tatiana Stefanova, email: tatiana.stefanova@hp.com.

> *Wir freuen uns, Ihnen mitzuteilen, dass wir seit kurzem eine neue Niederlassung in Moskau, Russland haben. Bei Anfragen wenden Sie sich bitte an Frau Tatiana Stefanova, E-Mail: tatiana.stefanova@hp.com.*

MC6 We are pleased to inform you that we have recently retained the services of Ms Tatiana Stefanova to assist with our sales in Russia. Ms Stefanova will start her duties on 1 September 2005. She will be working exclusively with Hewlett-Packard and only on the Russian market.

> *Wir freuen uns, Ihnen mitzuteilen, dass wir seit kurzem Frau Tatiana Stefanova zur Unterstützung unserer Verkaufabteilung in Russland eingestellt haben. Frau Stefanova wird Ihre Arbeit am 1. September 2005 beginnen. Sie wird ausschließlich für Hewlett-Packard arbeiten und nur auf dem russischen Mark tätig sein.*

MC7 We are delighted to advise you of the 100th anniversary of Reebok International Ltd. In the course of this event, please have a look at our website www.reebokstore.com for more than 100 special offers.

Wir freuen uns sehr, Sie auf das 100-jährige Bestehen von Reebok International Ltd. aufmerksam zu machen. Anlässlich dieses Jahrestages finden Sie mehr als 100 Sonderangebote auf unserer Website www.reebokstore. com.

MC8 We were shocked to hear about the sudden death of Ms Read and offer our condolences. She was a fine person who will be sadly missed by us. We have only the fondest memories of her. Please accept our deepest sympathies.

Wir waren schockiert, über den plötzlichen Tod von Frau Read zu hören und möchten Ihnen unser herzliches Beileid aussprechen. Wir haben sie außerordentlich geschätzt und werden sie sehr vermissen. Sie wird uns immer in guter Erinnerung bleiben.

Mit aufrichtiger Anteilnahme

20.4 Tasks

Please write emails using the following details and make use of the text components wherever you can:

20.4.1 Saturn, Germany to Microsoft Corp USA

- Betreff/Anrede
- Sie feiern am 1. Juni 2005 Ihr 25-jähriges Bestehen.
- In diesem Zusammenhang wollen Sie zwei Wochen lang mehrere Werbekampagnen mit Gewinnspielen und Sonderangeboten starten.
- Sie möchten nachfragen, ob Microsoft Corp. bereit ist, Software Ihrer Wahl zu absoluten Sonderpreisen für diesen Anlass anzubieten.
- Große Nachfrage besteht wie immer an *Windows XP* und an *Office Small Business Edition 2003*.
- Ferner möchten Sie wissen, ob Microsoft Corp. für diese Werbekampagnen auch Werbeträger wie Luftballons, Fähnchen etc. zur Verfügung stellt.
- Schlusssatz

20.4.2 Durable, Germany to Office Supplies, Saudi Arabia

- Betreff/Anrede
- Sie möchten mitteilen, dass Herr Neumann, der Gebietsleiter für den Verkauf Nahost, Ende des Jahres in Rente gehen wird.
- Sein Nachfolger, Herr Meyer, wird zur Zeit eingearbeitet.
- Sie planen für Anfang Oktober 2005 eine Geschäftsreise mit Herrn Neumann und Herrn Meyer nach Nahost, um Herrn Meyer seinen Stammkunden vorzustellen.
- Sie möchten wissen, ob ein Besuch bei Office Supplies angenehm wäre, und zwar möglichst vom 04. bis 07. Oktober 2005.
- Ankunft mit Flug LH4711 aus Frankfurt, am 04. Oktober 2005, um 13.30 Uhr.
- Rückflug am 07. Oktober 2005, um 09.00 Uhr.
- Sie erkundigen sich, ob Office Supplies zwei Hotelzimmer im „Sheraton Hotel" zu Corporate Rates[11] buchen kann und wie hoch die Room Rate ist. Ansonsten nehmen Sie die Hotelreservierung von Deutschland aus vor.
- Sie fragen, ob es möglich ist, die Herren vom Flughafen abholen zu lassen.
- Sie bitten um Bestätigung oder Vorschlag eines Ersatztermins.
- Schlusssatz

20.4.3 Fill in the missing prepositions

1. Congratulations … being appointed … the Purchasing Manager … Hewlett-Packard.
2. We wish you every success … this new position.
3. Please note that a site map and detailed directions will be found … www.twinings.com.
4. This is to inform you that Ms Jones is no longer employed … our company.

[11] Corporate Rate: Sondertarif für Geschäftsleute

5. Ms Hall is now … charge … customer support.
6. We are pleased to inform you that we have recently retained the services of Ms Tatiana Stefanova to assist … our sales … Russia.
7. She will be working exclusively … Hewlett-Packard and only … the Russian market.
8. We are delighted to advise you … the 100th anniversary of Reebok International Ltd.
9. Please have a look … our website www.reebokstore.com … more than 100 special offers.
10. We are planning a business trip … China to introduce Mr Smith … his key customers.

UNIT 21   APPLYING FOR A JOB

21.1 Key facts

An application consists of a <u>covering letter</u> and a CV (<u>curriculum vitae</u>[12]), in some countries also called a <u>résumé</u> (AE). Although online applications are becoming increasingly popular, they continue to take the form of a covering letter and a CV, <u>albeit</u> in electronic form. The purpose of your CV is to make you sound an interesting, prospective employee and thus be <u>shortlisted</u> for an interview.

Both the covering letter and the CV should be short, easy to read and convincing. Remember the *KISS*-principle – **K**eep **I**t **S**hort and Simple!

21.2 Presenting application documents

Make sure that your job application is convincing both visually and in terms of contents. This means:
- Presentation of your documents in attractive folders or clip files, eg as offered by Durable.
- Professional layout of your documents by using the Durable software for job applications.

For more information on job application folders and software, see <u>www.durable.de</u>.

21.3 Covering letters
21.3.1 Eight points for a successful covering letter

(1) Give your full contact details in the address header.

(2) Address your letter to someone personally, if necessary call the company to ask for a contact person in the personnel or human resources department.

(3) Say why you are writing and where you saw the <u>advert</u>, if available give a ref no.

(4) Summarise your experience, skills and achievements but do not repeat your CV.

(5) Show you have the skills asked for in the job advertisement.

(6) Say what you can do for the company and what your strengths are.

---

[12] curriculum vitae: Latin for life story

(7) Ask for an interview and mention when you are available for it.

(8) Ask for specific extra information on the job.

For more advice on writing covering letters, see www.business-spotlight.de/skills.

21.3.2 Model covering letter

(1) Susanne Fischer
Hermannstr. 2
50344 Köln, Germany
Tel. +49 221 360 287
email: susanne.fischer@gmx.de

(2) Mary Norman
Personnel Department
Reebok International Ltd
1895 J W Foster Boulevard
Canton, MA 02021
USA

July 15, 2005

Application for the position of customer service representative at Reebok International Ltd

Dear Ms Norman

(3) I am writing to apply for the challenging position of customer service representative at Reebok International Ltd that you recently posted on your Reebok website.

(4) As you will see from my curriculum vitae, I trained as an industrial clerk in a German company with <u>subsidiaries</u> all over the world. Therefore, I acquired a sound knowledge of international communication and organization. During my BA studies in Translation and Multilingual Communication at the University of Applied Sciences, Cologne I was able to strengthen my communication skills in English and Spanish.

(5) Having spent my <u>study-related internship</u> in the United States, I gained experience in tracking orders from the entry stage through completion. My specialization is communication and organization as evidenced by in my thesis entitled "Communication in the 21st Century". I like handling multiple tasks and working in a team environment.

(6) I believe that my qualifications and experience are ideally suited to helping RIL satisfy its customers. In particular, I believe my fluent language skills of German, Spanish and English would be of great benefit to RIL.

(7) I would welcome the opportunity to discuss my application personally in an interview at your convenience. Since I am ticketed for Boston from August 1 to August 29, 2005 I would be more than happy to come to Canton for an interview.

(8) I would like to confirm my strong interest in the above position and kindly ask you to send me a detailed description of the job advertised.

I look forward to receiving a positive response from you in the near future.

Sincerely yours
Susanne Fischer
Susanne Fischer

21.4 Curriculum vitaes

Different countries may have different <u>requirements</u> and styles of CVs or <u>résumés</u>. Therefore, the practise of each country should be followed.

In general, a CV or résumé should include the following details:

- Personal details
- Personal profile or statement (two or three sentences summarising your skills, strengths, hopes, and plans encouraging the employer to read the rest)
- Education (most recent education first)
- Work experience (most recent experience first)
- Interests
- Skills
- References

For more on CVs/résumés, see <u>www.soon.org.uk/cvpage.htm</u> or <u>http://www.cln.org/themes/writing_resumes.html</u>

21.4.1 Model curriculum vitae

Personal details	Susanne Fischer Hermannstr. 2 50344 Köln, Germany Tel. +49 221 360 287 email: susanne.fischer@gmx.de
Personal profile	Before my degree I strengthened my commercial and communication skills as an industrial clerk in an international company handling multiple tasks in a fast-paced team environment. My experience abroad improved my communication skills.

Education

2000-2003	University of Applied Sciences, Cologne, Germany Bachelor of Arts, Multilingual Communication in English and Spanish 4-month <u>placement</u> in Warwickshire, UK at Ford Motor Company
1998-2000	3-year-traineeship at Ford-Werke AG, Cologne, Germany Qualification as industrial clerk
1989-1998	Helmholtz Gymnasium, Bonn, Germany Major: English and computer science Minor: Spanish

Professional experience

| Since 07/2003 | **Freelance Translator**
Specialist fields: sporting events such as Formula 1, soccer, technical documents regarding car and truck technology
Clients: international companies |

Interests:	Bicycling, skiing, Formula 1, cars
Skills:	Good knowledge of French, basic knowledge of automotive technology, Microsoft Office, TRADOS and Wordfast (translation software)
References:	available on request

21.5 Placements (BE) or <u>internships</u> (AE) abroad

Many degree programmes provide for a semester abroad where a placement has to be completed. Also in this case, a <u>covering letter</u> and a CV have to be drafted.

21.5.1 Model application for a <u>placement</u> abroad

Susanne FischerHermannstr. 2 50344 Köln, Germany
Tel. +49 221 360 287 email: <u>susanne.fischer@gmx.de</u>

Twinings Ltd
<u>Personnel Department</u>
South Way
Andover
Hampshire
SP10 5AQ
Great Britain

15 July 2005

Dear Sir or Madam

I am writing to you to enquire about the possibility of completing a placement at your company.

I am currently studying *Multilingual Communication* at the University of Applied Sciences Cologne, Germany and I am required to do a four-month placement involving at least 20 hours per week in the fifth semester of our degree.

Having trained as an industrial clerk in an international company before my degree, my written and spoken English is fluent.

Additionally, I can handle correspondence in Spanish. I am also familiar with Microsoft Office.

I would be very grateful if you were able to offer me a placement from October 2005 onwards enabling me to gain experience of working abroad.
Please find enclosed my CV.
Should you require any further information, I will be happy to provide it.

I look forward to hearing from you soon.

Yours faithfully

Susanne Fischer
Susanne Fischer

21.6 Text components

JA1   I am writing to apply for the position of customer service representative at Reebok International Ltd that you recently posted on your Reebok website.

> *Hiermit bewerbe ich mich auf die Stelle als Kundendienstberaterin bei Reebok International Ltd., die Sie kürzlich auf Ihrer Reebok-Website ausgeschrieben haben.*

JA2   I am writing to you in response to your advert in *The Times* on 3 July 2005 and wish to apply for the above position.

> *Aufgrund Ihrer Anzeige in der Zeitung The Times vom 3. Juli 2005 möchte ich mich auf die o.g. Stelle bewerben.*

JA3   Your above vacancy is of considerable interest to me as it seems suited to my interests, experience and abilities.

> *Ihre o.g. Stellenausschreibung ist für mich von großem Interesse, da die Stelle genau meinen Interessen, meiner Erfahrung und meinen Fähigkeiten entspricht.*

JA4 I believe that my qualifications and experience are ideally suited to helping Hewlett-Packard expand its international operations.

Ich glaube, dass meine Fähigkeiten und meine Erfahrung bestens geeignet sind, um Hewlett-Packard bei der Expansion internationaler Unternehmen zu unterstützen.

JA5 I believe that I should be able to meet your needs since I have many years of experience as a translator.

Ich glaube, Ihren Anforderungen gerecht zu werden, da ich über eine langjährige Übersetzungserfahrung verfüge.

JA6 My specialisation is technical translations, and I have translated a wide range of manuals.

Mein Fachgebiet ist technische Übersetzungen. Ich habe schon viele Betriebsanleitungen übersetzt.

JA7 I am very much interested in working with Hewlett-Packard and am convinced that my technical knowledge would be of great benefit to your company.

Ich würde mich sehr freuen, bei Hewlett-Packard zu arbeiten und bin überzeugt, dass meine technischen Kenntnisse von großem Vorteil für Ihre Firma sein würden.

JA8 I would like to confirm my strong interest in a translating position at Hewlett-Packard and look forward to a positive response from you in the near future.

Ich möchte noch einmal mein großes Interesse an der Übersetzungsposition bei Hewlett-Packard zum Ausdruck bringen und würde mich über Ihre baldige positive Nachricht freuen.

JA9 I would very much like the opportunity to meet you personally to discuss my application further.

I am ticketed for London from 1 to 29 August 2005, should a personal interview be provided.

> *Ich würde mich sehr freuen, Sie persönlich kennen zu lernen und mit Ihnen meine Bewerbung näher zu besprechen.*
>
> *Ich bin in der Zeit vom 1.-29. August 2005 in London, falls ein persönliches Vorstellungsgespräch vorgesehen ist.*

JA10 I would be more than happy to come to London for an interview.

Should you require any further information, I will be happy to provide it.

> *Ich würde mich sehr freuen, zu einem Vorstellungsgespräch nach London zu kommen.*
>
> *Sollten Sie noch weitere Fragen haben, so stehe ich Ihnen sehr gerne zur Verfügung.*

21.7 Tasks

Spend time researching details about the job that interests you and information about the employer – their structure, products and business philosophy from one of the following sources:

- Company advertising, reports and publications
- Newspaper adverts
- The Internet

21.7.1 Write a covering letter using the results of the above research

21.7.2 Write a CV or résumé using the results of the above research

21.7.3 Fill in the missing prepositions

1. I am writing to apply … the challenging position … customer service representative … Reebok International Ltd that you recently posted … your Reebok website.
2. I am writing to you … response … your advert … *Boston Herald* … July 3, 2005 and wish to apply … the above position.
3. As you will see … my curriculum vitae, I trained … an industrial clerk … an international company.
4. During my BA studies I could intensify my communication skills … English and Spanish.
5. I believe that my qualifications and experience are ideally suited … helping RIL satisfy its customers.
6. … particular, I believe my fluent language skills … German and Spanish would be of great benefit … Hewlett-Packard.
7. I am also familiar … Microsoft Office and Wordfast.
8. I would welcome the opportunity to discuss my application personally … an interview … your convenience.
9. Since I am ticketed … Boston … August 1 … August 29, 2005, I would be more than happy to come to Canton … an interview.
10. I look forward … receiving a positive response … you in the near future.

UNIT 22   PRESENTING IN ENGLISH

22.1 Key facts

Self-confident, entertaining and casual. That's the way Anglo-American speakers arrest the attention of the audience. What's the key to their success?
We will focus on simple techniques for making a good impact.

22.2 Structure

In fact, Anglo-Americans use a special way of presenting material. The overriding principle is: *follow a clear structure*! It is helpful to think of a presentation as consisting of the following three parts:

Part I	The introduction
Part II	The main part
Part III	The conclusion

22.3 Part I   Introduction

An Anglo-American introduction is <u>subject to</u> a clear structure. It indicates what **will** be discussed. Below is a guideline for a good introduction:

Step 1	Engaging the audience
Step 2	Welcoming
Step 3	Showing appreciation
Step 4	Introducing yourself
Step 5	Introducing the topic
Step 6	Highlighting the reason for the topic
Step 7	Structuring
Step 8	Using visuals
Step 9	Timing
Step 10	Handling questions
Step 11	Leading up to the main part

Step 1   Engaging the audience
Get the audience's immediate attention by engaging them with effective openings. According to communication experts, the first three minutes

of a presentation are the most important ones. Therefore, engage your audience as follows:

1. Tell a personal anecdote, eg *"What happened to me lately was ..."*
2. Show a picture, a caricature, a cartoon.
3. Refer to a topical issue from the TV or newspaper, eg *"Whilst having breakfast this morning, I read in the newspaper that ..."*
4. Ask a rhetorical question, eg *"What do you think are the greatest challenges in our industry?"*
5. Quote an interesting statement by somebody or a proverb.
6. Go back in history, eg *"20 years ago, we ...."*
7. Make a provocative assumption, eg *"If we go on like this, ..."*

Step 2   Welcoming

Thank the audience for being there. They will feel welcome from the first moment and this will have a positive impact on the atmosphere.

Good morning everybody. Thanks for coming.
First of all, let me thank you all for coming here this morning.
I'm very pleased that so many of you could come this morning.

Step 3   Showing appreciation

Appreciate the expenditure of time. The audience will warm to the speaker and feel that the preciousness of their time is well appreciated.

I know that you are all very busy and I appreciate your coming this morning.
I know that you are all involved in time-consuming projects.
I am aware that coming here involved postponing your normal work.

Step 4   Introducing yourself
Who is the speaker?

Tell the audience who you are. This includes both your name and your function or position within the company. Anglo-Americans like to know a bit about the person speaking.

> *I'm ...*
> *My name is ...*
> *For those of you who do not know me already, I'm ...*
>
> *I'm responsible for ...*
> *I'm in charge of ...*
> *As you know, I'm the Sales Manager.*

Step 5   Introducing the topic
What is the topic of the presentation?

Tell the audience what you are going to be talking about. Many participants are late or came in at last minute, ie they are not focussed.

Repeat the topic to make sure everybody has got it.

> *This morning I'd like to talk about ...*
> *What I want to present you this morning is ...*
> *Today's topic is ...*

Step 6   Highlighting the reason for the topic
Why is everybody here?

Give the audience a good reason for being there and you will get their full attention. If the topic has an influence on their business they will be interested.

> *My presentation is of great importance for you because ....*
> *Being aware that you'll all have to deal with this matter in the near future, my presentation will show you how to handle ....*
> *Today's topic is of special interest for those of you who ...*

Step 7   Structuring
When will the different parts of the topic be treated?
Give the audience a clear guide by dividing your topic into subtopics.
This procedure guarantees transparency and comprehensibility.
The overriding principle is: *KISS*-**K**eep **I**t **S**hort and **S**imple!
Consider the magical figure of three when structuring your presentation.
A quantity of three is easy to remember and therefore often found in
abbreviations of companies, eg IMB, BMW, UPS, etc.

> *Firstly, ..., secondly, ...and thirdly ...*
> *We'll begin by ..., then we'll go on to ...; and finally,*
> *we'll discuss ...*
> *I'll start by ..., next I'll go on to ...; and I'll finish by ...*

or

> *I've divided my presentation into three parts ...*
> *I'll concentrate on three major issues ...*
> *I'll be focussing on three points ...*

Step 8   Using visuals
How will the topic be got across?
Most people are the visual type. The audience will look forward with
anticipation to the use of visuals.

> *I'll be relying mostly on overheads to help illustrate my points.*
> *I'll be illustrating my presentation with some charts and diagrams*
> *that I prepared for you earlier.*
> *I'll be using PowerPoint slides to accompany my presentation.*

or

> *My presentation analyses the current market trend researched by ...*
> *I've based my presentation on the proposal of ...*
> *Since statistics show that ..., I've based my presentation on the*
> *latest figures of ....*

Step 9   Timing
How long does the presentation take?

Remember the <u>standard gauge</u> of 20-30 minutes makes the best possible use of the audience's attention span.

From our childhood, we are used to absorbing knowledge within a fixed time-frame, eg lessons at school, seminars, work-shops, etc. Thus, we are able to adjust to the time stipulated.

> *My presentation is going to take up about 30 minutes of your time this morning.*
> *It'll last about 30 minutes to cover my points.*
> *My presentation will take about 30 minutes.*

Step 10   Handling questions
When should you answer the audience's questions?

Inform the audience during the introduction **when** they may ask you questions.

Generally, in formal presentations, questions are answered after the presentation to avoid the speaker <u>losing the plot</u> or control of the time frame.

Sometimes, however, at informal presentations or work-shops, questions are dealt with during the presentation.

Inviting questions **after** the presentation:

> *Perhaps we can leave your questions until the end of my presentation.*
> *I'd like to ask you to hold your questions till the end.*
> *There will be plenty time left over for questions at the end of my presentation.*

Inviting questions **during** the presentation:

> *If you have any questions, don't hesitate to ask.*
> *Feel free to ask your questions as we go along.*
> *Don't hesitate to ask questions during my presentation.*

Step 11   Leading up to the main part
How can you lead up to the main part of a presentation?

Make use of a <u>transition</u>. It is just one short sentence to show the audience where you are and to signalise that the introduction part is finished.

> *If you all agree, I'll start with my first point.*
> *After having clarified all organisational points, I'd like to begin with point 1, ...*
> *After having introduced you extensively, let's come to the first point, ...*

22.4 Task part I

Take a company of your choice and prepare an introduction of a presentation in accordance with the eleven steps mentioned before. Focus on the following three major points:

- Brief company history
- Traditional product range
- A brand-new product

22.5 Part II   Main part
How can you structure the main part?

In general, the main part should be logical and easy to follow. Once again a clear structure is vital. The main part should consider the following essential steps:

Step 1	Reporting on a major point
Step 2	Signalling the end of a section
Step 3	Summing up a point
Step 4	Leading up to the next point

Step 1   Reporting on a major point
Fewer facts - more stories.

Our brains can remember the development of events more easily than just a sequence of simple facts. In order to report convincingly on a major point you should consider the following:

- Divide your major points into subtopics. Remember the magical figure of three, three subtopics is the perfect number.
- The subtopics must relate to the topic of the presentation.
- The order of the subtopics must be logical.
- <u>Transitions</u> link the subtopics.
- Make use of rhetorical questions. It is often more interesting to present your ideas as questions rather than direct statements. Questions involve the audience and make your presentation sound more conversational, eg *"Did you know that …"*
- Make your audience listen with the *"What … is"*-technique, eg *"What I'm saying is… "*

Step 2   Signalling the end of a section
Show the audience where you are.

Before finishing a point, however, you should indicate the end of the section.

That is all I have to say about …   *This just about brings me to the end of the first point.*   *That's about all for point one.*

Step 3   Summing up a point

Work with concise repetitions. They are essential, especially at the end of a point in the main part. Short repetitions make it easier for the audience to memorise content. When summarising, the audience is given the information in clear and concise bits.

To sum it all up, …   *In a nutshell, …*   *To put it more simply, …*

Step 4   Leading up to the next point
Link the different points in the main part by using transitions.

> *... which brings me to the end of point one, namely ...*
> *This leads me nicely into my second point ...*
> *Now I'd like to focus on my third point ...*

Steps 1 to 4 can be repeated as often as required depending on the number of major points. After summarising the last major point, however, a <u>transition</u> to the conclusion has to be made.

22.6 Task part II

Work out the main part of your presentation in accordance with the four steps mentioned before.
Focus on the following three points:
- Brief company history
- Traditional product range
- A brand-new product

22.7 Part III Conclusion

Finish strongly! The audience retains best the information it received last. Therefore, a strong conclusion is important and should consist of the following five steps:

Step 1	Signalling the end of the main part
Step 2	Summing up
Step 3	Giving a personal view (optional)
Step 4	Thanking
Step 5	Inviting questions

Step 1   Signalling the end of the main part

Inform the audience that all major points have been discussed now and that you want to come to the end of your presentation.

> *Now I'm coming to the end of my presentation.*
> *I've almost finished my presentation.*
> *So, that was my last point, and I'm now approaching the end of my presentation.*

Step 2   Summing up

Make a final summary repeating briefly what was discussed.

When presenting in English, concise repetitions are essential. The Anglo-American audience is accustomed to being informed in this way. Consequently, although having summed up the major points in the main part, a final summary in the conclusion has to follow.

> *Before I stop, let me briefly highlight the major points once again.*
> *In conclusion, I'd like to point out once more ...*
> *I'd like to conclude with a brief summary of the most important facts.*

Step 3   Giving a personal view

Give your personal opinion or make a forecast.

The forecast of a presentation is optional. It is a new point of view given on the basis of what **was** discussed. The forecast could be considered as the speaker's last chance to influence the opinion of the audience.

> *In my view, ...*
> *I'm absolutely certain that ...*
> *So, how is all of this relevant to us?*

Step 4   Thanking
Thank the audience for listening.

Thank you for your attention.
I'd like to thank you all for your attention.
Thanks for coming.

Step 5   Inviting questions
Initiate the question and answer session.

Are there any questions you'd like to ask? I'll be happy to answer them now.
Do any of you have any questions? If so, I'd be happy to answer them right now.
I've done all the talking so far, now it's your turn. Are there any questions left?

22.8 Task part III
Work out the conclusion of your presentation in accordance with the five steps mentioned before.

22.9 Golden rules
1. Start strongly!
Plan the beginning of your presentation very thoroughly and memorise it.
2. Keep eye contact with the audience!
If you have to turn towards a flipchart, board or other, stop talking until you have found the figure or graph you want to refer to. Then turn to face the audience again and continue with your presentation.
3. Be brief!
Go straight to the point. Keep the content clear and concise.
4. Speak as freely as possible!
Try to memorise your concept as far as possible. Only glance at your manuscript to aid your memory.

5. Use your voice!

Speak loudly, clearly and slowly! Pause at appropriate places! Vary the speed of your speech! Make use of the rise and fall of your voice!

6. Turn your presentation into a conversation!

Use rhetorical questions and try to make your presentation more conversational.

7. Use body language!

Use your hands, facial expression or gestures to underline your arguments!

8. Make your presentation entertaining!

Think of some jokes or funny comments to put a smile on the audience's face.

9. Develop your own way of doing things!

Don't copy other speakers. Develop a style that makes *you* feel comfortable.

10. Finish on a strong note!

Look at the audience and finish slowly and clearly. Pause for a little while for the message to sink in, before thanking the audience for their attention.

UNIT 23   CONDUCTING A MEETING

23.1 Key facts

Nowadays, meetings are common practice in every company. Communication at meetings must be clear and well structured in order to be effective. We will focus on the following three parts:

Part I   Opening a meeting
Part II   Making a statement
Part II   Closing a meeting

23.2 Part I   Opening a meeting

The opening should consider the following essential steps:

Step 1   Signalling the beginning of the meeting
Step 2   Welcoming
Step 3   Introducing yourself
Step 4   Highlighting the reason for the meeting
Step 5   Referring to the agenda
Step 6   Timing
Step 7   Checking preparation
Step 8   Taking the minutes
Step 9   Leading up to item 1

Step 1   Signalling the beginning of the meeting
The <u>chairperson</u> opens the meeting.

OK, let's get started. *Ladies and Gentlemen, I think we should begin.* *Now that everybody is here, let's begin.*

Step 2   Welcoming
Create a good atmosphere with a friendly welcome.

> *First of all, I warmly welcome you to our team meeting today.*
> *Welcome to our meeting today.*
> *I'm happy to welcome all of you today.*

Step 3 Referring to the agenda
What's on the agenda?
Tell the participants the points that **will** be discussed today. Refer to the agenda on your handout, projected on a wall or written on a flip chart, etc.

> *As you will see from the handout in front of you, today's first item on the agenda is dealing with ...*
> *Item 2 is concerned with ...*
> *and item 3, our last item on the agenda, is focussed on ...*

Step 4 Timing
How long will the meeting last?
Tell the participants how long the meeting is expected to take.

> *The meeting will last approx two hours.*
> *I've scheduled 30 minutes for each item, so we should be ready in one and a half hours.*
> *This meeting won't last more than two hours.*

Step 5 Introducing yourself
Who is in the chair?
In case you are not known to all the participants introduce yourself and tell the participants that you will be chairing the meeting today.

> *My name is ... and I am in charge of ... I'll be chairing the meeting today.*
> *For those of you who do not know me, my name is ... and I am responsible for ... I'll preside over the meeting this morning.*
> *Let me briefly introduce myself. I'm ... and I'm the head of the marketing department. I'll be in the chair this afternoon.*

Step 6   Highlighting the reason for the meeting
Why is everybody here?
Give the participants a good reason for being there to engage their interest.

Today's meeting will be very important to you because ...
I don't have to remind you how important this meeting is, since we all have to live with the decisions that will be taken today.
Since you'll all have to deal with point 1 of today's agenda soon, today's meeting is of particular importance for you.

Step 7   Checking preparation
Has everybody got the material or settled the to-do list?
Make sure everybody has got the necessary documents or done the preparatory work. Usually, the progress made on the to-do list decided on at the last meeting is checked by the <u>chairperson</u> of the meeting.

Before we start, let me make sure you all got my invitation and the to-do list of the last meeting. I hope you all found the time to prepare ...?
Before we go into the subject let me ask you if you all settled the to-dos?
Did you all get my email? You have had sufficient time to prepare ...? John, have you prepared the latest figures regarding ...

Step 8   Taking the minutes
Who is writing the minutes?
Before starting on the main subject, clarify who is going to <u>take the minutes</u>. Generally, at regular meetings with the same group of participants, each person takes it in turn to write up the minutes in brief form and then mails it to all participants the next day.

Who's going to take the minutes today?
Who is today's <u>minute-taker</u>?
Bill, my assistant, has kindly agreed to take the minutes. Please make sure we will all get the minutes by email tomorrow.

Step 9   Leading up to item 1
How to lead up to the first item on the agenda?

Make use of a short <u>transition</u>. It is just a short sentence to signalise that you are going into the subject now.

> *Well, let's come to the first item on the agenda which is …*
> *OK, let's start with item 1 on the agenda.*
> *Now, I'd like to begin with item 1, namely …*

23.3 Part II   Making a statement

If opinions are collected at a meeting there is generally little time to prepare a concise two-minute-statement regarding your opinion on an issue, a proposal or an objection.

The key to success is using the following steps:

Step 1   Introducing yourself (optional)
Step 2   Introducing the topic
Step 3   Structuring
Step 4   Summing up
Step 5   Giving a personal view
Step 6   Leading up to other opinions

The <u>chairperson</u> may initiate collecting opinions as follows:

> *John, let's begin with you. What do you think about …?*
> *Would you like to comment, David?*
> *I would like to give the floor to Susan.*

In order to avoid upsetting other participants and provoking time-consuming discussions you should take care to express objective statements in a neutral tone of voice.

Step 1   Introducing yourself
Who makes a point?
Step 1 is optional and depends whether you are known to the participants or not.

> *(My name is Tom Jackson.) As head of the marketing team, I would like to comment on ...*
> *In my function as Sales Director, I think I'm entitled to object ...*
> *Since this item has already been discussed in our team before, I would like to propose ...*

Step 2   Introducing the topic
How do you think about the topic?
Tell the participants what you think about the topic.

> *The new marketing strategy seems very interesting, because ...*
> *As interesting as this new product range may be, we should consider ...*
> *From the financial side I can't agree to this new investment, because ...*

Step 3   Structuring
What points of view are to be expected?
Give the participants a clear guide.

> *First of all, this new marketing strategy requires ...*
> *My next concern is ...*
> *This is connected to the point I just made. Whilst I am sure that ..., I have every confidence that ...*

Step 4   Summing up
What are the major points to consider?
Make a very brief final summary repeating the most important facts.

In a nutshell, ...
To sum up, ...
In other words, ...

Step 5   Giving a personal view
How is all of this relevant to us?
Express your personal opinion or make a forecast.

In my view, ...
I'm absolutely certain that ...
Based on the present state of affairs, I think that ...

Step 6   Leading up to other opinions
What do the others have to say on this?
Finish your statement by expressing interest in the views of other participants.

Well, that's my take on it from a sales perspective. I would welcome your views on ...
Well, that's my view of things from the financial side. I would like to hear where the others stand on this issue.
As I've just mentioned, that's what I think about the issue, but I would like to hear your comments.

23.4 Part III Closing a meeting

The <u>chairperson</u> closes the meeting officially. Closing a meeting should be made in accordance with the following steps:

Step 1	Signalling the end of the meeting
Step 2	Summing up
Step 3	Giving a personal view (optional)
Step 4	Dealing with the to-dos (optional)
Step 5	Closing the meeting
Step 6	Thanking

Step 1   Signalling the end of the meeting

Tell the participants that all major parts have been discussed now.

> *This brings me to the end of our meeting.*
> *I must bring our meeting to order. We are over time. If nobody has any objections, I'd like to postpone item 4 until our next meeting.*
> *Let's come to an end.*

Step 2   Summing up

Briefly sum up the results of the meeting.

> *So, let me just <u>recap</u> on the results of our meeting.*
> *I'd like to make a brief summary of the items we discussed this morning.*
> *Let me briefly summarise the items we agreed on this morning.*

Step 3   Giving a personal view

This step is optional. Depending on the topic being discussed, the <u>chairperson</u> might like to give a personal opinion.

> *In my view, ...*
> *I'm convinced that the outcome of this meeting will ...*
> *I am confident that the results of today's meeting will ...*

Step 4   Dealing with the to-dos

This step is optional, too. If necessary, nominate a participant/ participants to deal with the to-dos.

> *John, I'd like to nominate you to deal with the to-dos.*
> *John and Susan, I'd like to nominate you both to deal with the to-dos by our next meeting.*
> *We'll deal with the to-dos as usual, ...*

Step 5   Closing the meeting
Close the meeting.

> *I think we have covered everything. Let's close the meeting.*
> *If nobody has anything to add, let's bring the meeting to a close.*
> *If there are no more questions, I'd like to close the meeting. The next meeting will be on 18 October 2005.*

Step 6   Thanking
Thank the participants for their time and cooperation.

> *Thank you for your time and cooperation.*
> *I'd like to thank you all for your constructive contributions.*
> *Thanks for coming.*

23.5 Task
Business role play:
Suppose you are working as a manager for Reebok International Ltd, USA and you have been invited by the Managing Director to a meeting of all the heads of department in order to discuss **how to increase the awareness of your products on the European market**. You have been requested to talk the matter over with your team and to submit a concrete proposal at that meeting.

You have to take into consideration:
- The best ways of achieving this aim
- Whether your proposal is effective, and represents good value for money
- Who your competitors on the European market are and what their policy is

The participants are as follows:
1. The Managing Director, who will chair the meeting
2. The Communications Manager
3. The Financial Controller
4. The Personnel Manager
5. The Production Manager
6. The Marketing Manager
7. The Sales Manager
8. The Public Relations Manager
9. The R&D Manager
10. The IT Manager

GLOSSARY

ENGLISH	GERMAN
account	Konto
acknowledgement	Auftragsbestätigung
Act of God	Höhere Gewalt
act upon (to)	abhandeln
addressee	Empfänger
adhere to (to)	etw. einhalten
adjustments	Einstellungen
advert	Anzeige
airfreight company	Luftfrachtgesellschaft
airway bill	Luftfrachtbrief
albeit	obgleich
annul (to)	annullieren
applicable fees	anfallende Gebühren
appreciate (to)	etw. begrüßen
arrange a meeting point (to)	einen Treffpunkt vereinbaren
ask for extension (to)	um Zahlungsaufschub bitten
assortment	Sortiment
at any rate	auf jeden Fall
at your disposal	zu Ihrer Verfügung
at your expense	auf Ihre Kosten
balance sheet	Bilanz
bales	Ballen
bank details	Bankangaben
barrels	Fässer
batch (to)	bündeln
Bill of Lading	Seefrachtbrief, Konnossement
block letters	Briefe in Blockform
bulk payment transfer messages	Weiterleitung von gesammelten Zahlungsaufträgen
bumpy	unruhig
business conduct	Geschäftsgebaren
call on so.(to)	jmdn. besuchen
cancel (to)	stornieren
cash discount	Skontoabzug
caution marks	Vorsichtsmarkierungen
Certificate of Origin	Ursprungszeugnis
chairperson	Leiter eines Meetings
change arrangements (to)	Vereinbarungen ändern

ENGLISH	*GERMAN*
circumstances beyond our control	Umstände außerhalb unserer Kontrolle
clean B/L	reines Konnossement
clean on-board B/L	reines An-Bord-Konnossement
collection	Zahlungseinzug
collection agency	Inkassoagentur
commercial invoice	Exportrechnung
commercial value	Handelswert
complaints	Beschwerden
complimentary close	Schlussformel
confirm arrangements	Vereinbarungen bestätigen
consignment	Sendung
consignment note	Frachtbrief
continuation page heading	Briefkopf einer Folgeseite
convenient	passend, gelegen, geeignet
correspond to (to)	entsprechen
counter offer	Gegenangebot
Country of Origin	Ursprungsland
courtesy copy	Gefälligkeitskopie
covering letter	Bewerbungsschreiben
credit (to)	gutschreiben
credit agency	Auskunftei
credit enquiries	Kreditanfragen
credit limit	Kreditgrenze
creditworthiness	Kreditwürdigkeit
crossed cheque	Verrechnungsscheck
curriculum vitae	Lebenslauf
customs clearance	Zollabfertigung
debit (to)	belasten (Konto)
delay in delivery	Lieferverzug
delivery date	Liefertermin
delivery reminder	Liefererinnerung
despatch advice message	Versandanzeige
despatch department	Versandabteilung
dimensions	Abmessungen
draft	Tratte (gezogener Wechsel)
draw a cheque on a bank (to)	einen Scheck auf eine Bank ausstellen
drums	Trommeln
due amount	fälliger Betrag
effect payment (to)	Zahlung vornehmen

ENGLISH	*GERMAN*
enclosures	Anlagen (bei Briefen)
enquiries	Anfragen
equipment failure	Betriebsstörung
evidence	Beweis
exceed (to)	überschreiten
exempt from	ausgenommen von
exhibit (to)	ausstellen
expiry	Ablauf
export credit insurance	Exportkreditversicherung
export reference book	Export-Nachschlagewerk
extension number	Durchwahl
factoring	Factoring (Gesellschaft, an die Rechnungen abgetreten werden können)
factory tour	Betriebsrundgang
failure	Ausfall, Defekt
faulty	fehlerhaft
faulty workmanship	fehlerhafte Verarbeitung
features	Besonderheiten, Eigenschaften
financial standing	Finanzlage
find a ready market (to)	guten Absatz finden
flush with the left margin	linksbündig
for customs purposes only	nur für Zollzwecke
Force Majeure	Höhere Gewalt
forwarding agents	Spediteur
freight	Fracht
from stock	ab Lager
full information	ausführliche Informationen
full punctuation	vollständige Interpunktion
fund up (to)	Geldmittel zur Verfügung stellen
General Terms and Conditions	Allgemeine Geschäftsbedingungen
genuineness	Echtheit
get down to business (to)	zum geschäftlichen Teil übergehen
glimpse	Eindruck
goods inward test	Wareneingangskontrolle
goods receiving department	Warenannahme (Abteilung)
goodwill	Kulanz
govern (to)	regeln, bestimmen
guarantee (BE)	Garantie
hand over (to)	übergeben

ENGLISH	*GERMAN*
hold so. responsible for sth. (to)	jmdn. für etw. verantwortlich machen
hospitality	Gastfreundschaft
in duplicate	in doppelter Ausfertigung
in transit	auf dem Transportwege
in triplicate	in dreifacher Ausfertigung
inconvenience	Unannehmlichkeiten
incorporate	etw. angeben
indelible	abriebfest
induce (to)	veranlassen
insist on (to)	bestehen auf
insolvency	Insolvenz
insurance policy	Versicherungspolice
International Chamber of Commerce	Internationale Handelskammer
internship (AE)	Praktikum
invoice	Rechnung
irremovable	nicht zu beseitigen
irrevocable	unwiderruflich
irrevocable and confirmed documentary letter of credit	unwiderrufliches und bestätigtes Dokumentenakkreditiv
issuance of L/C	Eröffnung eines Dokumentenakkreditivs
last bid	letztes Angebot
launch (to)	etw. neu auf den Markt bringen
legal effect	rechtliche Auswirkungen
Letter of Credit	Akkreditiv
letterhead	Briefkopf
liable for sth. (to hold so.)	(jmdn. für etw.) haftbar machen
lose the plot (to)	den Faden verlieren
main carriage	Hauptbeförderung
make arrangements (to)	Vereinbarungen treffen
maturity date	Fälligkeitsdatum
means of payment	Zahlungsmittel
minute-taker	Protokollführer
mode of transport	Transportart
modify (to)	verändern
notification	Mitteilung, Bescheid
oblige (to)	hier: entgegenkommen; gefällig sein
observe (to)	etw. einhalten

ENGLISH	GERMAN
on presentation of	bei Vorlage
on stock	auf Lager
open punctuation	offene Interpunktion
order confirmation	Auftragsbestätigung
order form	Auftragsformular
outstanding for payment	zur Zahlung ausstehen
overdue	überfällig
overdue accounts	überfällige Verbindlichkeiten
packing list	Packliste
patterns	Muster
payment behaviour	Zahlungsmoral
payment reminder	Zahlungserinnerung
pick so./sth. up (to)	jmdn./etw. abholen
placement (BE)	Praktikum
political upheaval	politische Umwälzungen
poor quality output	schlechtes Produktionsergebnis
port of destination	Bestimmungshafen
port of shipment	Verschiffungshafen
post code (BE)	Postleitzahl
premises	Firmengelände
process (to)	bearbeiten
proforma-invoice	Proforma-Rechnung
purchase (to)	kaufen
purchase prices	Einkaufspreise
quotation	Angebot
quote (to)	ein Angebot unterbreiten
raise an invoice (to)	eine Rechnung ausstellen
raw material	Rohmaterial
ready for shipment	versandbereit
recalculate (to)	überdenken, neu kalkulieren
recap (to)	kurz wiederholen
reciprocate (to)	sich erkenntlich zeigen
recollect (to)	sich erinnern an
reference initials	Bezugszeichen
regulations	gesetzliche Vorschriften
reliable	zuverlässig
remittance	Überweisung
replacement material	Ersatzmaterial
requirements	Bedarf
respite	Zahlungsaufschub
résumé (AE)	Lebenslauf
revocable	widerruflich

ENGLISH	*GERMAN*
riot	Volksaufruhr
safeguard (to)	absichern
sales tax	Verkaufssteuer
salutation	Begrüßung
sample	Probe
seafreight	Seefracht
secure email support	Service für verschlüsselten E-Mail-Versand
ship's rail	Reling des Schiffs
shipment	Versand
shipping company	Reederei
shipping marks	Versandmarkierungen
shortage in weight	Fehlgewicht
shortfalls	Fehlmengen
shortlisted (to be)	in der engeren Wahl sein
signature block	Unterschriftsabschnitt
significant orders	größere Aufträge
solicitors	Rechtsanwälte
spare parts	Ersatzteile
special discount	Sonderrabatt
standard gauge	Richtmaß
stroll	Bummel
study-related placement (BE)	studienbegleitendes Praktikum
subject line	Betreffzeile
subject to (to be)	unterliegen
subject to prior sale	Zwischenverkauf vorbehalten
submit (to)	unterbreiten
subsidiaries	Niederlassungen
substitute	Ersatz
take leave (to)	sich verabschieden
take the minutes (to)	Protokoll führen
terms of delivery	Lieferbedingungen
terms of payment	Zahlungsbedingungen
the pleasure is mine	ganz meinerseits
tight with time (to be)	wenig Zeit haben
total value	Gesamtwert
trade references	Handelsreferenzen
transition	Übergang
turnover	Umsatz
unclean B/L	unreines Konnossement
under separate cover	mit separater Post

ENGLISH	*GERMAN*
unearned cash discount	unberechtigter Skontoabzug
unit price	Einzelpreis
unsaleable	unverkäuflich
vessel	Schiff, Frachter
way bill	Frachtbrief
will meet with your approval	wird Ihnen gefallen
with utmost confidentiality	streng vertraulich
zip code (AE)	Postleitzahl

DEVELOPMENT IN COMMERCIAL CORRESPONDENCE

	TRADITIONAL	*MODERN*
1. Form of Communication	approx 90% letters, approx 10% faxes and emails	approx 90% emails, approx 10% faxes and letters
2. Layout	mixed forms (indented form, semi-block form)	block form
3. Punctuation	full punctuation	open punctuation
4. Style	very formal	less formal, more personal, short and precise
5. Date	1st May, 2nd June, 3rd July, Monday, 17th August (BE) May 1st , June 2nd , July 3rd , Monday, August 17th (AE)	1 May, 2 June, 3 July, Monday 17 August (BE) May 1, June 2, July 3, Monday, August 17 (AE)
6. Attention line	placed **under** the inside address of a company: For the attention of Mr. Ory FAO Mr. Ory Attention: Mr. Ory	placed **before** the company name: Mr Ory Reebok International Ltd
7. Salutation in letters, emails, faxes	Miss Mrs. Mr. Dear Sirs (BE) Gentlemen: (AE)	Ms (if married or unmarried) Mr Dear Sir or Madam (BE) Ladies and Gentlemen (AE) Dear Jim (both BE and AE)
8. Endings	**Looking** forward to hearing from you soon.	We **look** forward to hearing from you soon.
9. Complimentary close in letters, emails, faxes	Yours faithfully (BE) Yours sincerely (BE) Yours truly (BE) Yours very truly (BE) Very truly yours (AE) Cordially yours (AE) Sincerely (AE)	Best regards (BE) Yours faithfully (BE) Best regards (AE) Sincerely (AE)

10. Use of abbreviations	little use	much use
11. Vocabulary	inquiry dispatch cc = carbon copy	enquiry despatch cc = courtesy copy

NB: Although there is a great difference between the "traditional" and the "modern" usage of layout, punctuation, date, <u>salutation</u>, endings, <u>complimentary close</u>, and vocabulary, it must be said that both "traditional" and "modern" styles are still in use in commercial correspondence. However, there is a strong tendency to use the modern style nowadays.

DIFFERENCES IN BRITISH ENGLISH AND AMERICAN ENGLISH

acknowledgement	acknowledgment
apologise (to)	apologize (to)
authorise (to)	authorize (to)
bank holiday	public holiday
centre	center
cheque	check
colour	color
computerise (to)	computerize (to)
consignment note	way bill
curriculum vitae	résumé
dialled	dialed
favour	favor
favourable	favorable
focussing	focusing
gauge	gage
guarantee	guaranty
have a look at sth. (to)	take a look at sth.(to)
holiday	vacation
honour (to)	honor (to)
labelled	labeled
lift	elevator
memorise (to)	memorize (to)
mobile (NEVER handy)	cell phone
organise (to)	organize (to)
placement	internship
post code	zip code
programme (program is for computer programs only)	program
realise (to)	realize (to)
specialisation	specialization
standardise (to)	standardize (to)
summarise (to)	summarize (to)

Expressions of time:

ten *past* five	ten *after* five
Monday *to* Friday	Monday *through* Friday
at the weekend	*on* the weekend

on the phone:	**on the phone**
0= oh	*0= zero*

COMMON ABBREVIATIONS IN FOREIGN TRADE

ABBREVIATION	*MEANING*
am	ante meridiem; in the morning
ad	advertisement
AE	American English
asap	as soon as possible
attn	attention
B/L	Bill of Lading
BE	British English
C/O	Certificate of Origin
CAD	Cash Against Documents
cc	courtesy copy/carbon copy
Corp	Corporation
CV	Curriculum Vitae
D/A	Documents Against Acceptance
eg	exempli gratia; for example
EC	European Community
EFTA	European Free Trade Association
enc	enclosure
est	established
ETA	Expected Time of Arrival
ETS	Expected Time of Shipment
FAO	For the Attention Of
FYI	For Your Information
HGV	Heavy Goods Vehicle
ie	id est; that is to say/in other words
Inc	Incorporated
L/C	Letter of Credit
lb	libra; pound (measurement of weight)
Ltd	Limited company
MS	Motor Ship
OEM	Original Equipment Manufacturer
pm	post meridiem; in the afternoon
Plc	Private limited company
pls	please
SS	Steamer Ship
thx	thanks
TOU	Terms Of Use (Microsoft)

BIBLIOGRAPHY

I Books consulted

ASHLEY, A., (1994): *A Handbook of Commercial Correspondence.* Oxford: Oxford University Press

ASHLEY, A., (2003): *Oxford Handbook of Commercial Correspondence – New Edition.* Oxford: Oxford University Press

BEETHAM TILLEY, Sally/ADAIR, Justin (1997): *Business English Activities.* Stuttgart: Ernst Klett Verlag für Wissen und Bildung GmbH

BOSEWITZ, René/KLEINSCHROTH, Robert, (2003): *Getting through at meetings.* Reinbek bei Hamburg: Rowohlt Taschenbuch Verlag

BOSEWITZ, René/KLEINSCHROTH, Robert, (2001): *How to communicate effectively - verstehen und verstanden werden im Business.* Reinbek bei Hamburg: Rowohlt Taschenbuch Verlag

BOSEWITZ, René/KLEINSCHROTH, Robert, (2002): *Idioms at work - bessere Geschäfte mit treffendem Englisch.* Reinbek bei Hamburg: Rowohlt Taschenbuch Verlag

CHAPMAN; Rebecca, (2003): *English for Emails.* Berlin: Cornelsen Press GmbH & Co. KG

CHRISTIE, David, (2003): *New Basis for Business - Pre-Intermediate.* Berlin: Cornelsen Press GmbH & Co. KG

CROWTHER-ALWYN, John (1997): *Business Roles- 12 simulations for Business English.* Cambridge, UK: Cambridge University Press

EVANS, David, (1997): *Decisionmaker - 14 business situations for analysis and discussion*. Cambridge, UK: Cambridge University Press

FISCHER, Roger/URY, William/ PATTON, Ury (1999): *Getting to Yes*. London: Penguin Books Ltd.

GEISEN, Herbert/HAMBLOCK, Dieter/POZIEMSKI, John/ WESSEL, Dieter (2002): *Englisch in Wirtschaft und Handel*. Berlin: Cornelsen Press GmbH & Co. KG

GRILL, Wolfgang/PERCZYNSKI, Hans, (2004): *Wirtschaftslehre des Kreditwesens*. Troisdorf: Bildungsverlag EINS, Verlage Gehlen, Kieser, Stamm, Wolf

HAUFE VERLAG GMBH & CO. KG, (2003): *Die 100 wichtigsten Geschäftsbriefe in Englisch*. Planegg bei München: Haufe Verlag GmbH & Co. KG

INDUSTRIE UND HANDELSKAMMER IN NORDRHEIN-WESTPHALEN, (2004): *Praktische Arbeitshilfe Export/Import*. Bielefeld: W. Bertelsmann Verlag

INTERNATIONAL CHAMBER OF COMMERCE, (2000): *Incoterms 2000 - ICC official rules for the interpretation of trade terms*. Köln: ICC Deutschland-Vertiebsdienst, Internationale Handelskammer

JONES, Leo/ALEXANDER, Richard (2003): *New International Business English*. Stuttgart: Ernst Klett Sprachen GmbH

KLARER, Mario (2003): *Präsentieren auf Englisch*. Frankfurt/ Wien: Wirtschaftsverlag Carl Ueberreuter

LAHRMANN, Nils, (2003): *Bewerben im Ausland*. Hamburg: CC-Verlag

BIBLIOGRAPHY

(?.) LAWS, Anne, (2004): *Meetings*. Oxford: Summertown Publishing Ltd.

MAC KENZIE, Ian, (2002): *English for Business Studies*. Cambridge: Cambridge University Press

POWELL, Mark (2002): *Presenting in English - how to give successful presentations*. Boston, MA, USA: Thomson/Heinle Corporation

RICHARD, Willi/ MÜHLMEYER, Jürgen/ WEFERS, Guido/ BERGMANN, Bernhard, (2004): *Betriebslehre der Banken und Sparkassen*. Rinteln: Merkur Verlag

SACHS; Rudolf/ABEGG, Birgit (2001): *Commercial Correspondence - Englische Handelskorrespondenz für die Praxis*. Ismanning: Max Hueber Verlag

II Internet links

Allgemeine Kreditversicherung AG
http://www.allgemeine-kredit.de

Alltea, UK
http://www.allteas.com

Anschriften der weltweiten Handelskammern- Handelsbeziehungen, Wirtschaftsnachrichten
http://www.worldchambers.com

Apple Comp. Inc., USA
http://www.apple.com

Ausstellungs-und Messeausschuss der Deutschen Wirtschaft e.V. (AUMA), Inlands- und Auslandsmessedaten, Informationen zum Messeauftritt
http://www.auma.de

BfD Der Bundesbeauftragte für den Datenschutz
http://www.bfd.bund.de/informationen/info2/info2094.htm

Bundesagentur für Außenwirtschaft (BfAI)
http://www.bfai.com

Bürgel Wirtschaftsinformationen GmbH & Co. KG
http://www.buergel.de

Business Spotlight
http://www.spotlight-verlag.de

Denholm shipping services
http://www.denholm-shipping.co.uk/

Deutscher Factoring-Verband e.V.
http://www.factoring.de

Dunhall, UK
http://www.dunhall.co.uk

Durable, Germany
http://www.durable.de

Englishweb Korrespondenz
http://www.englishweb.de/korrespondenz/business_email.php

Euler-Hermes-Kreditversicherungs-AG
http://www.eulerhermes-kredit.com

Europäischer Dachverband der Industrie- und Handelskammern
http://www.eurochambers.com

Factoring
http://www.globalfinanceonline.com/factoring.html

BIBLIOGRAPHY

Factoring-Team, Beratung und Vermittlung
http://www.factoring-vermittlung.de/4650.html

Finanzierung: Factoring als Alternative
http://www.impulse.de/the/fin/157495.html

GCSE Business and Communication Systems,
parts of a business letter
http://www.lw-chameleon.co.uk

Gerling Kreditversicherung AG
http://www.gerling.com/credit

Hewlett-Packard
http://www.hp.com

Hunt & Palmer International, UK
http://www.huntpalmer.co.uk

Industrie- und Handelskammern in Deutschland
http://www.ihk.de

Institut für Auslandsbeziehungen (IFA)
http://www.ifa.de

International Chamber of Commerce Deutschland (ICC)
http://www.icc-deutschland.de

KCI Reader-Based Writing Style Guide, letters
http://www.kanten.com/styleguide/pdfs/blop.pdf

Magazin für Außenwirtschaft
http://www.localglobal.de

Messekalender Deutschland
http://www.messekalender.de/

Microsoft, USA
http://www.microsoft.com

Punctuation
http://www.bradford.ac.uk/acad/civeng/skills/punctuan.htm

Reebok, USA
http://www.reebok.com
http://www.reebokstore.co.uk/stores

Shipping and ports, UK
http://www.dft.gov.uk/stellent/groups/dft_shipping/documents/
sectionhomepage/dft_shipping_page.hcsp

Successful CV resumes
http://www.soon.org.uk/cvpage.htm

SWIFT
http://www.swift.com/index.cfm?item_id=2325

Tim Berners-Lee
http://www.w3.org/People/Berners-Lee/
http://www.tbwt.com/views/specialrpt/special%20report-1_11-29-99.asp

Transworld Systems, debt collection agency
http://www.transworldsystems.net/pastdue.html

Twinings, UK
www.twinings.com

United Nations Commission on International Trade Law (UNCITRAL),
Informationen zum Internationalen Handelsrecht
http://www.uncitral.org

Walter-Eucken-Schule, Karlsruhe
http://walter-eucken-schule.de/lehrer/rohrmann/english_corresponde
nce%20contents.htm

Weltbank, Informationen zu Ländern und Regionen
http://www.worldbank.org

Welthandelsorganisation
http://www.wto.org

Weltweite Geschäftskontaktbörse
http://www.e-trade-center.com

Wirtschaftsdatenbanken mit Firmenprofilen und Marktbeobachtung
http://www.genios.de

III Online Dictionaries

Axone Financial Glossary
http://www.glossary.axone.ch/ViewTerm_test.cfm?TID=633

Encyclopedia
http://www.encyclopedia.com

LEO – Link Everything Online
http://www.dict.leo.org/

Yale University Library
http://www.library.yale.edu/

IV Other

Magazines:
Business Spotlight – *English for International Communication*
Editions 2003/2004